BARRON'S

GUIDE TO GRADUATE BUSINESS SCHOOLS

12th Edition

by
Eugene Miller

Executive-in-Residence and Professor
Florida Atlantic University
Former Vice Chairman
USG Corporation
Former Senior Vice President
New York Stock Exchange

BARRON'S

For Thelma, Ross, Scott, June, Paul, and Alan

The GMAT practice exam beginning on page 29 of this book is reprinted from Barron's *How to Prepare for the GMAT,* 12th edition, by Eugene D. Jaffe, M.B.A., Ph.D., and Stephen Hilbert, Ph.D., 2001.

All inquiries should be addressed to:
Barron's Educational Series, Inc.
250 Wireless Boulevard
Hauppauge, New York 11788
http://www.barronseduc.com

Library of Congress Catalog Card No. 89-640070 (ISSN 1043-190X)

International Standard Book No. 0-7641-1488-3

PRINTED IN THE UNITED STATES OF AMERICA
9 8 7 6 5 4 3 2 1

Table of Contents

Preface

Of all the degrees given at the master's level, probably none are more popular today than graduate business degrees, the most popular of these being the MBA. Since 1950, the MBA alone has been awarded to about 1 million graduates. The popularity of these degrees in recent years is indicated by the burgeoning enrollments at graduate schools of business and the sharp increase in the number of institutions that offer them. Today, such degree programs are offered by 750 colleges and universities. Since 1970, the number of master's degrees awarded each year in business administration has soared from 21,000 to around 100,000. Currently, about 275,000 students are enrolled in MBA programs. Of these students, about two-thirds are men and one-third are women. More than 60 percent of all MBA students go to school part time.

In many fields of business, possession of a graduate business degree is a prerequisite to being hired. While there has been some growing criticism of the effectiveness of MBA programs in preparing their students for the real world of business, most business schools are dealing with these complaints by making changes in their programs. A growing number of major companies that have management development and training programs hire only such graduates. Some business firms even encourage promising middle management employees to attend evening or weekend programs by paying all or part of their tuition expenses.

With so many universities now offering graduate business degrees, the job of selecting the right school is a difficult one. The purpose of this guide is to help you sort out the key elements that go into making a sound choice. Therefore, in addition to providing general guidelines for evaluating the various schools, we have provided you with factual and insider's information about each business school. We hope it will take some of the complexity and confusion out of selecting the right graduate business program for you. The business schools listed in this guide either are accredited by the AACSB or have regional accreditation.

I would like to extend my special appreciation to Dr. Neuman Pollack, professor at the College of Business, Florida Atlantic University, a contributing editor of this book, and to my research assistants, Paul M. Gottlieb, Ross Miller, June Miller Blitz, and Dr. Scott Miller.

Part I

GETTING INTO GRADUATE BUSINESS SCHOOL

Why Go to Graduate Business School?

How to Choose a Business School

The Largest Enrollments

The Application Procedure

Taking the GMAT—A Sample Exam

Financing Your Education

What Employers Seek

Why Go to Graduate Business School?

Going to a graduate school of business is a considerable investment of time and money. For a full-time student, the cost will be anywhere from $30,000 to $90,000 for two years of study. A part-time student may expect to pay less, but he or she will have to spend as many as four years or more to complete the degree.

Despite the cost and time involved, a growing number of students feel that attending graduate business school is worthwhile. About 275,000 students are enrolled in MBA courses. Each year 100,000 or more students receive a master's in business—more than any other advanced degree except for the master's in education. Applications for admission to graduate business schools continue to increase.

Why is a master's in business, and the MBA in particular, so popular? The main reason is that it is so highly regarded by the business world. Business firms are anxious to hire these graduates, and they are willing to pay higher salaries to those who have the degree. In a growing number of major firms that have extensive management development programs, such programs are open only to those with a relevant master's.

Businesses are concentrating more and more on these graduates because they find that graduate business training gives them valuable background and sophistication in business subjects. Companies have discovered that these graduates learn new jobs more quickly, are able to shoulder responsibilities sooner, and earn promotions faster than those lacking graduate business preparation. Therefore, with a variety of candidates having business backgrounds to choose from, many business firms would rather hire someone with a master's in business than someone with only an undergraduate degree in business. Talk to the personnel directors of many large firms, and they will point out that those with a master's in business not only can move into initial jobs easily but also have the skills and background necessary to learn new fields and deal with new business techniques and strategies. The complexity of business has increased enormously in recent years. Growth of multinational corporations and the radical changes brought about by computers, and the emphasis on total quality management are important new developments on the business scene, and these are usually part of the curriculum of any graduate business school. Graduate business students also learn the latest theories in finance, organizational structure and behavior, marketing theory, international trade, and dozens of other subjects that have immediate or future application in the business world. Companies want people with backgrounds that include such knowledge.

Companies are also willing to pay a premium for those with a graduate business degree. Starting salaries for those holding master's degrees in business administration often average $15,000 to $60,000 a year more than for those who graduate with just a bachelor's degree. In some cases, if you go to a prestigious graduate business school, job offers can run as much as $75,000 a year more than what you would receive with only a bachelor's degree in business.

Statistical records on the achievements of these students are still sketchy, so it is difficult to determine how all do financially or employment-wise over a period of time. However, some business schools do keep track of their graduates' job success. Twenty-five years out of school, one third of the Harvard MBAs are CEOs, managing directors, partners, or owners of companies. Obviously, Harvard is not a typical business school. However, even though most other business schools cannot boast of such a record, most placement directors can cite dozens of their graduates who have moved into top jobs in business. In a recent *Business Week* magazine list of the 1,000 largest companies in the United States, over 25 percent of the chief executive officers had MBAs.

Looking at a master's in business from a student's point of view, here are the advantages:

- The courses give you a broad background and training in business skills and sophisticated business skills.

- In a tight job market, you might have an advantage in finding a job that a person with only a bachelor's degree does not have. (It is important to keep in mind that the better the business school you attend, the better your chances of getting a job and at higher pay.)

- The odds are substantial that you will get a higher starting salary than you would with only a bachelor's degree.

- If you are interested in being chosen for a management development program by any of the country's top corporations, it is very advantageous to have a relevant master's (usually from a leading business school).

- If you are interested in going into your own business, you will find that your graduate courses will help you very much in your own business.

- If you are interested in getting chosen for a "fast track" program at some companies—which permits you to bypass or speed through the typical entry-level jobs—you will find a master's degree quite useful in most cases.

- Minority group members will find many companies anxious to locate and hire them for managerial positions if they have completed a graduate business program. Most companies are under great pressure from federal government agencies to increase the number of minority group employees in their management ranks. These firms intensively recruit minority students with graduate business degrees.

- Business is under considerable pressure to hire women for managerial posts, and companies are looking mainly for those with graduate business degrees. Currently, more than one third of all MBA students are women. Women who have graduate business degrees will find job and pay opportunities much better today. This doesn't mean that women will get paid the same as men holding identical degrees, but they will have greater job leverage than they have had before. Part of the current difference in starting pay between male and female graduates may result from job experience. Many men have had several years of prior work experience, and business firms are willing to pay more for this extra experience.

- Getting a graduate business degree at night or through distance learning is often a valuable alternative for individuals who find themselves stifled in their present situations. It can help them move out of dead-end jobs in their present firms, or into growth positions with other firms.

- If you aren't seeking a career in the business world, but plan a career in law, health administration, public administration, or a variety of other fields, possession of an advanced business degree and the knowledge it represents can be valuable. Even in creative fields or health care, a growing number of people desiring to become managers of opera companies or art museums find this training helpful. This is one reason more students are deciding to take joint programs that combine the study of business with that of law, architecture, or other disciplines. In 1998 more than 40 universities offered a master's degree in arts management.

- There are also a growing number of situations where "career changers," individuals who decide they want to make a major career change in their 30s and 40s, are enrolling as MBA students. A number of doctors, lawyers, and other professionals, as well as artists and teachers, have decided that entering the business world is a smart move.

Your Degree

MASTER OF BUSINESS ADMINISTRATION (MBA)

Most graduate schools of business award the MBA degree, but many schools award other graduate business degrees. Some of these degrees are equivalent to the MBA, while others are not. For example, the Master of Science in Management (MSM) awarded by the DuPree College of Management at Georgia Institute of Technology is considered the equivalent of an MBA in terms of program requirements. However, there are a variety of master's-level business degrees that aren't considered equivalents, and these are discussed in the following section. If you are interested in an MBA-type program, don't be confused by degree programs that sound similar but actually are not.

Basically, most full-time MBA programs are designed to be two-year courses of study that give students a broad background in a wide range of business subjects. MBA programs usually require students to take a substantial number of core courses in basic business areas such as accounting, finance, marketing, and management. MBA candidates also take other required general and specialized courses in business and are often permitted to take electives from the business school curriculum or from that of other schools within the university. In terms of credits, the MBA program usually requires from 36 to 60 semester hours. Students with strong undergraduate business backgrounds may be able to finish an MBA program by taking as few as 30 credit hours. (Most other master's degrees offered by business schools are either degrees that require fewer courses than the MBA or degrees that are quite specialized.) Only a handful of schools grant the MBA after only one year's graduate study. But there seems to be a trend in that direction as costs of getting an MBA grow. Notre Dame,

Babson, Pittsburgh, Rollins, Kellogg, University of Georgia, and Pepperdine are among the more than 20 schools that offer one-year MBA programs. Texas A & M has a 16-month program.

Specific degree requirements vary from school to school. Some programs require the student to take only specified courses, while others grant considerable leeway in the courses each student can select. The same is true of research requirements and examinations at the completion of the course work. A large number of schools require a student to pass either an oral or a written comprehensive examination before he or she is eligible for the degree. Some schools require that each student submit a thesis.

The thesis represents a considerable body of research and usually counts as six hours of credit. It provides the opportunity for intensive study of a problem selected by the student, who then works under the supervision of a faculty adviser or committee. At many schools, course work is submitted in lieu of a thesis requirement.

Also, many schools require that students earn a minimum grade-point average of B (3.0 on a 4.0 scale). Other schools require them to show proficiency in various fields or topics related to the study of business. For example, at Boston University, computer and information systems is a required part of the curriculum. There is generally a time limit on how long a student can take to finish any graduate business degree; this usually varies from five to seven years.

As a potential MBA student, you should study the differences in program requirements very carefully. If you think that writing a thesis would be too difficult an undertaking, concentrate on those schools that don't require one. You should also see if the school is strong in the business field you are most interested in. For example, the University of Illinois and Wharton are outstanding in accounting. Kellogg is a leader in marketing. MIT and Carnegie Mellon are leaders in production and operation management; Thunderbird, NYU, and University of South Carolina in international business; and Wharton, Chicago, and NYU in finance. Babson is a leader in entrepreneurship. The University of Texas offers 15 courses in entrepreneurship. If you are interested in getting your MBA as quickly as possible, look into those schools whose degree requirements are less demanding.

The same careful study of graduation requirements is important for those who plan to get their degrees as part-time students. It normally takes at least three to five years to earn on MBA on a part-time basis. This means that the number of required courses is an important consideration in determining the length of time you will have to attend school to earn your degree.

ALTERNATIVES TO THE MBA

The MBA is a very popular degree, but it isn't the only worthwhile one. There are other graduate business degrees, such as the Master of Science in Business (MSB) or the Master of Science in Business Administration (MSBA), which can usually be earned with only 30 hours of course work. This type of alternative program may give you the business courses you want without forcing you to take additional courses required by the MBA. Master's degrees are also offered in a variety of business subjects like accounting and management science. Such programs are undertaken by those students who want to concentrate in a specific field and are not interested in the broader requirements of the MBA.

While the great majority of degrees awarded are MBAs, here are some of the special business- or management-related master's programs offered in addition to the MBA. For example, the

Master of Science in Operations Research (MSOR) offered by Michigan State University emphasizes the utilization of quantitative methods for the modeling, analysis, control, and optimization of business and engineering systems. The University of California at Los Angeles (UCLA) has a Master of Science in Management (MSM) program that prepares students to conduct substantial research in management science. The Master of Science in Accounting (MSA) degree at DePaul University offers a heavy concentration in accounting. The University of Southern California offers a Master of Business Taxation (MBT) or a Master of Accounting (MAcc). The University of Denver has an International MBA and a Master of Taxation (MT) through its law school. Fordham University in New York offers an MBA in Communications and Media Management. The Stuart School at Illinois Institute of Technology (IIT) now offers an MS in Financial Markets and Trading, an MS in Environmental Management, and an MS in Marketing Communications. Carnegie offers an MS in Electronic Commerce.

In 2000 more than 12,000 students received their graduate degrees in public administration. This increasingly popular alternative to the MBA is finding favor with students seeking professional positions in various levels of government. Many public administration programs throughout the country have changed their curricula to include more business skills materials.

Basically, the degrees just mentioned are for those students who already know what field of business they want and who desire a more specialized business education. The disadvantage of those degree programs is the fact that most companies seeking job candidates with a well-rounded business education want MBA graduates, not those with the more specialized master's degrees. Also, although the MBA commands a sizable salary differential over a bachelor's degree in business, the same differential is not always commanded by the master of science degree in business or its equivalent. However, some special degrees, like the Master in Taxation, are in heavy demand.

SPECIAL PROGRAMS

Joint MBA Programs

If you are interested in combining business training with another professional discipline, a growing number of universities offer MBA programs (and sometimes other master's in business degrees) in conjunction with other professional degrees. The major advantage here is that the combined programs usually enable a student to save both time and money. For example, the combined MBA/JD (business/law) degree program takes four years of full-time study; separately, the programs would normally take five years.

Probably the MBA/JD is the most popular combined program, and this is offered by several dozen universities, including Michigan, Pennsylvania (Wharton), Columbia, Virginia, Stanford, Harvard, Cornell, Chicago, Washington (St. Louis), and Boston. But there are other combination programs as well, and one may be perfectly suited to your career needs. Several schools offer MBAs combined with architecture and urban planning. Columbia Business School has a three-year program with its School of Architecture that grants a degree in urban planning along with the MBA. At Washington University, there are joint MBA/MSW (social work) and MBA/MArch programs. Boston University offers an MBA in combination with a Master of Science in Manufacturing Engineering. Columbia offers the MBA combined with journalism, and the Wharton School (University of Pennsylvania) offers the MBA/MSE (engineering) among other programs. Boston also offers an MBA/MS in Television Management with the School of Public Communication and an MBA/MA in Economics with the Graduate School. The University of Michigan has initiated joint degree programs with the Institute of Public Policy Studies (MBA/MPP), the Music School (MBA/MM), and 14 other schools or units within the university. Washington University also offers an MBA/MA Eastern Asian Studies degree. The University of Chicago has added a joint degree program in the physical sciences. A decade ago, 10 graduate business schools made an arrangement with several nursing schools to offer a joint MBA/MSN degree program. Some of the graduate business schools taking part are Michigan, Texas, Virginia, Vanderbilt, and Columbia. Dartmouth's Tuck School and Medical School offer a joint MBA/MD program. Each year, the number of joint programs increases.

The actual structures of the combined programs vary widely. For instance, take the business/law program. At many schools you spend the first year in law school, then go to business school for the second year. You then take the third and fourth years in the law school while squeezing in some business courses during these two years. In other joint programs, each semester offers almost equal numbers of business courses and courses in the other degree field.

The major advantage of the joint program, as indicated earlier, is that it can be completed in a shorter time than by taking the two degree programs separately. However, by pursuing a joint program, you might find yourself becoming academically overqualified for your career needs. An MBA is advantageous for a lawyer if he or she plans to go into corporate work. However, an individual might find it better to go to law school, decide on what legal specialty he or she wants, and then pursue a graduate business degree part time if it will be helpful in the chosen field of concentration. Before deciding on a joint program, it is wise to discuss it with prospective employers.

Still another problem with some of the joint programs is the fact that you usually have to apply and be admitted separately to each of the graduate schools. In other words, if you want to get into a joint MBA/JD program you will have to be admitted to both the law school and the business school separately. This means that if you are contemplating going into a joint program, you will have to do more planning when you are a college senior. Since it is difficult now to gain admission to law schools, you might have to send out a great many applications. Also, since law school is the harder school to get into, the quality of the business school you attend will be determined by the law schools that accept you. If you were going to business school alone, you might have a chance to be admitted by a number of leading ones, but if you can only get into a mediocre law school, chances are that the university's business school may also be mediocre.

For part-time students, a joint MBA program seems out of the question because of the great amount of time involved. On a part-time basis a joint program might run as long as 10 years, and few schools would encourage a part-time student to get involved in such a long-range undertaking.

Foreign Study

If you would like to combine graduate business study at a foreign university with study at an American business school, you will find a number of programs that offer foreign study. The reason is that most American graduate business programs are only one or two years long, and schools want to provide the complete program rather than share it with a foreign university where there may be substantial problems of coordination and supervision of programs between campuses located thousands of miles apart.

However, a substantial number of graduate business schools do offer programs that involve study abroad. For example, the Wharton School has exchange programs of one semester each. Students go in the fall semester to the London Business School, the Delft (Holland) Graduate Management School, the Institut Supérieur des Affaires in Paris, Stockholm School of Economics, or Universidad de Navarra at Barcelona. There is an MBA program at the Graduate School of Business Administration at New York University in which second-year students study one term at any one of 17 schools in 12 countries. The University of Chicago and Cornell University have long-standing, formal exchange programs, and the University of California at Berkeley, the University of Washington, and the Tuck School at Dartmouth College also have exchange programs. Washington now has 14 exchange partners in 13 countries. The Kellogg Graduate School of Management at Northwestern participates in 12 exchange programs with European and Asian graduate schools and also offers global issues courses that culminate in two-week trips abroad to meet business leaders in the country or region studied. Boston University has a management development program in Kobe, Japan, where selected MBA students may complete specific MBA course work. The University of Hawaii has a cooperative program with the Institute for International Studies and Training in Fujinomiya, Japan, and an exchange program with Keio University's Graduate School of Business in Yokohama, Japan. At the University of California at Berkeley, students can spend the fall term of their second year at one of eight leading business schools abroad. A number of U.S. graduate business schools are members of the Programme International de Management to facilitate exchange programs with business schools worldwide.

Dartmouth now offers an exchange program with the International University of Japan, which has recently established an MBA program in Niigata, Japan. The program, taught in English, is the first such business school in Japan and has been modeled after the program at Tuck.

The University of Michigan now has 14 different foreign exchange programs. The University of Chicago has recently opened a campus in Singapore and already has one in Barcelona.

Interestingly, Arthur D. Little, the management consulting firm in Cambridge, Massachusetts, has the accredited Arthur D. Little School of Management, which offers an 11-month Master of Science in Management degree to a class that is usually 90 percent international, typically representing dozens of countries.

Actually, most of these foreign study programs are mainly for those students who have already decided upon their careers and feel it is to their advantage to be able to speak a foreign language fluently, get to know a foreign country fairly well, and be aware of the special business practices and philosophies of a specific foreign country. Usually, though, students don't have overseas work as their career goal. For them, spending time at a university overseas may provide an interesting experience, but it could lengthen the time needed to get the graduate business degree. Also, it is often true that the student usually does not have access to the same business courses he or she would have by completing all graduate business work at an American business school. So, for most students, the disadvantages of such programs seem to outweigh the advantages.

Nevertheless, a small but growing number of American students want to study abroad part time or full time and receive their degree from a graduate business school overseas. They are not interested in the typical exchange program between an American graduate business school and a foreign graduate business school. For example, enrollment of U.S. students at the London Business School made up over 15 percent of its MBA class of 2000.

These students may have such an interest because they plan to live and work abroad or because their families are living overseas, and it is convenient to attend a local graduate business school. One interesting development is that a few American schools have started satellite schools overseas. For example, St. Xavier College in Chicago has an executive MBA program in Paris. This way students living abroad can get an American-type MBA program.

Obviously, the first choice for foreign students living abroad would be a business school in their own country or in a nearby country. Enrollments at foreign business schools are increasing, and many of these graduate business schools have achieved outstanding reputations.

Americans wishing to attend foreign business schools should be aware that if courses are not taught in English, they should be fluent in the foreign language used. Also, many foreign business schools charge considerably more tuition for overseas students than for residents of their own countries. For example, the London Business School charges over two times more tuition for overseas students than for those from Great Britain and the European Economic Community (EEC) countries. The same is true at Canada's York University, which has an outstanding graduate business school. Tuition there is about three times as much for non-Canadians as for Canadian residents. However, even with this premium, the cost at York is not high compared to major competitive U.S. schools.

Executive Programs

Executive programs are designed for those who already have middle management jobs and, generally, the endorsement and financial backing of their employers. A big advantage of these executive programs is that often students can complete the program in two years of study or less—a good deal shorter than the usual four years it takes to earn the degree as a part-time student. Students in executive programs are generally considered full-time students and take about the same courses as students in the regular MBA programs. Today over 180 colleges offer such programs and more than 10,000 students are enrolled in executive MBA programs.

In most schools, enrollment in the executive MBA programs is limited to outstanding middle management men and women between the ages of 30 to 45 who are sponsored by their firms. The cost of these programs—generally paid for by the employer—is usually a flat fee that includes tuition, books, and meals on campus. A typical program is the one at Fairleigh Dickinson, which is designed to handle a group of 25 students who go through the two-year program as a group in which they develop close working relationships.

Normally, an executive program has the same curriculum as a university's regular MBA program, except that some electives are eliminated. In a number of these programs, students spend the first week or two in September going to school full time. After that they have classes all day Friday of one week followed by all day Saturday of the next week. Or, they may go to class both Friday and Saturday of alternate weeks. This means that the employer must let them take one day of work off every two weeks, and the employee must give up one Saturday every two weeks.

The University of Chicago is considered the pioneer in the executive program, having started its own program more than 50 years ago. Over 4,500 executives have received degrees in this program. Among the graduate business schools offering an executive program are those at Rochester, Columbia, Wake Forest, Southern Methodist (Cox School), Pittsburgh, Pace, Illinois (at its Urbana-Champaign campus), New Mexico, Denver (Daniels), Northwestern (Kellogg), and the University of Washington.

If you can get in on an executive program, by all means do so. By selecting you for an executive program your company has shown that it feels you are promising enough to warrant investing a substantial amount of money in furthering your education. And you will be going to class with an elite group of students who may turn out to be valuable future business contacts and social acquaintances.

The executive programs discussed above lead to MBA degrees, and they should not be confused with another type of executive program that is also becoming popular.

These executive programs are usually one or two weeks in duration and are given by graduate business schools for company executives. They are usually tailored by the graduate school and the sponsoring company to meet the specific needs of the sponsor corporation. For example, USG Corporation has sponsored a one-week course on strategic planning at the Kellogg School of Management at Northwestern.

Today, over 140 graduate business schools offer these courses that are sponsored by a growing number of companies. General Motors, in particular, has been a major sponsor of such courses and has sent its executives to a number of graduate business schools.

A few graduate schools have built excellent facilities to hold these courses and house the executives. For example, the James L. Allen Center at Northwestern, in addition to classrooms, has attractive sleeping room accommodations, as well as dining facilities, athletic facilities, and most of the other amenities available at a small hotel.

Doctoral Programs

While most students who attend graduate business school are interested only in earning an MBA or other master's degree, some go on to earn their doctoral degrees. These can include the traditional Doctor of Philosophy (PhD), the Doctor of Business Administration (DBA), the Doctor of Commercial Science (DCS), and the Doctor of Professional Studies (DPS). Over 1,200 doctoral degrees in business were awarded in 2000, 30 percent of which were earned by women. If you are considering a doctoral degree program, here are some facts to keep in mind:

- A doctoral degree usually takes twice as long to earn as a master's, and sometimes the MBA is not the logical path to follow toward the doctorate.

- Earning a doctoral degree involves far more than taking additional courses and spending a longer period of time in school. Many schools require that their doctoral candidates be proficient in statistics, and students usually have to pass comprehensive tests in this area. Often, proficiency in a foreign language is required.

- You probably will have to take comprehensive oral and written examinations in three or more fields of business to demonstrate that you have an overall grasp of these areas.

- You must write a research dissertation, which can easily run 200 to 500 pages and take one or two years to write. Even after you've finished writing the dissertation, you have to defend it before a faculty committee, and this can be an awesome hurdle for some students.

Because getting a doctoral degree is a very difficult task for most graduate students, many schools discourage a student from trying to earn a doctorate unless they feel that he or she has the necessary scholastic abilities and plans to go into the academic world or some research field after graduation. One area of major demand for PhDs is for teachers at graduate business schools. While salaries in the academic world usually don't compare to what is available in the business world, salaries have increased. It is estimated that there is currently a PhD vacancy rate of 7 percent at business schools. Starting salaries for instructors or associate professors with a PhD can run $45,000 to $90,000 for a nine-month year. Many professors with specialties like finance or accounting earn annual salaries of $80,000 to $130,000; some "superstar" professors earn as much as $150,000 a year. A great deal of "raiding" has taken place lately as graduate business schools vie for top talent. Several years ago, Wharton wooed away a professor from Princeton for a package estimated at $250,000 a year. Professors also can supplement their teaching income with consulting work. Consulting fees of $1,000 to $4,000 a day are possible for outstanding specialists. Business schools face a shortage of qualified teachers. While business school enrollments have grown sharply since 1985, the number of new doctoral graduates has increased only by a very small amount. One reason is that it has been estimated that it costs $180,000 to $250,000 in extra tuition and lost income to gain a doctoral degree in business.

Only a few schools encourage business-oriented students to take the doctoral program. Pace University, for example, offers a doctoral program in business that is designed for qualified executives who want to experience a rigorous study program while continuing their professional careers. This program has been considered unusually successful.

Another key point to consider in evaluating the pros and cons of a doctoral degree is that there may be very little difference between what some companies would pay, for example, an MBA applicant and an applicant with a doctorate. In fact, in some cases a company might shy away from hiring a young job candidate with a doctorate who wants to get into a regular management training program. Companies often feel that doctoral applicants are overqualified or simply too academically oriented. If you want a business career, a doctoral degree may not do very much to help you get a job or speed your pay and promotion.

On the positive side, there are some jobs in the business world where the doctorate is regarded as a plus—particularly jobs in the economic and business research fields. Investment banking firms over the past five years have been hiring PhDs from the academic world at very high salaries. In recent years, an increasing number of newly minted PhDs in Business have opted for careers in the business world. Also, you might be the sort of person who wants the prestige, self-satisfaction, and joy of learning that one can get by undertaking such a course of study. If that's what you want, go full steam ahead.

A fairly recent development is the hiring of so-called "clinical professors" by a number of business schools. These professors are recruited from the ranks of corporate executives and the goal is to bring more real world business experience into the classroom. These clinical professors usually don't have the same academic credentials as their colleagues nor are they usually on the typical tenure track. More often they sign three- or five-year contracts and are rarely asked to do formal research. However, they often are full time and participate in most faculty activities.

How to Choose a Business School

There are a number of things you should consider when choosing a business school. Obviously, your range of selectivity depends on such factors as your undergraduate grades, the type of program you wish to pursue, whether you plan to go to school full time or part time, and your finances. If you live in a small city where there is only one university that offers a graduate business program, and you want to go to school in that city, your decision is somewhat limited. If you want to go to school in New York City, however, you have a choice of 10 or more schools that offer graduate business programs. In the Chicago area, there are over 20 schools offering the MBA program. If you are a good student with the financial resources to go to any school in the country, you have an even more difficult choice to make. A major new factor in the decision to go to graduate business schools is the increasing number of schools offering MBAs through "distance learning" courses. The sections that follow describe some of the criteria you should consider when deciding on your preference in schools.

Factors to Take into Account

ACCREDITATION

When you evaluate a school, accreditation is an important consideration. Accreditation is the process of recognizing educational institutions whose performance and integrity entitle them to the confidence of the educational community and the public. Accreditation of business schools usually comes about through two types of organizations.

The first type of accreditation group is a regional non-governmental or voluntary organization. Currently, there are six major regional organizations: the Middle States Association of Colleges and Schools (MSACS), the New England Association of Schools and Colleges (NEASC), the Northwest Association of Schools and Colleges (NASC), the North Central Association of Colleges and Schools (NCACS), the Southern Association of Colleges and Schools (SACS), and the Western Association of Schools and Colleges (WASC). These organizations establish criteria, evaluate institutions at their request, and extend approval to those colleges and universities whose purposes, resources, and performance the pertinent accrediting organization feels deserve such recognition.

Most universities are accredited by one of these six major regional groups. For you, this accreditation is a guarantee that the university, of which the business school is a part, has met the minimum standards set by the accrediting organization. In practical terms, it also means that, if you transfer from an accredited school, the chances are good that another school will accept your transfer courses and grades. If you transferred from a school that was not accredited, chances of getting credit for most of your previous work would be slim.

In addition to these regional organizations that provide general accreditation, there are accreditation groups set up to accredit specialized schools in areas such as architecture, journalism, med-

icine, and business. There are currently 37 professional fields where there are recognized accreditation agencies. In the business school area, the accreditation agency is the American Assembly of Collegiate Schools of Business (AACSB), now called the International Association for Management Education.

One very good yardstick to measure the quality of a graduate business school is to determine whether it is accredited by AACSB. Founded in 1916, AACSB is dedicated to furthering the quality of education at schools of business. It does this through an accreditation program at both undergraduate and graduate schools of business. As of December 2000, AACSB had accredited the master's degree programs at 376 of the more than 750 schools offering the MBA degree or its equivalent in the United States.

Just about all the major graduate schools of business have their programs accredited by AACSB, and many who lack accreditation are busily seeking it. To be accredited, a school must conform to a high level of standards. Up until 1982, these standards were pretty rigidly defined. For example, at least 75 percent of the faculty had to have their terminal degrees (usually the doctorate), and student-faculty ratios and the number of part-time and full-time faculty members were also precisely defined. In 1982, the AACSB made a sweeping revision in its accreditation standards to give its evaluators more leeway in judging the quality of a school's programs. The changes were adopted to reduce reliance on purely quantitative factors. In 1991, AACSB made some radical changes in their accreditation standards. These were the result of a two-year study by AACSB members and in response to criticism that there should be more flexibility in the accreditation process and more emphasis on teaching and preparing students for the needs of the business world.

Under the new standards schools have flexibility in determining their mission, or market niche, and to develop programs to accomplish their goals. They have more freedom to package their courses and to assemble faculty.

This new flexibility as applied to faculty means they are freer to use faculty members who have doctorates in fields other than business and that some professors may need only master's degrees as long as they have relevant professional experience.

On the other hand, there is emphasis on student standards, and students must be able to demonstrate skills in written and oral communications, quantitative analysis, and computer usage.

Many schools have already made changes in their curriculum to match the new requirements, but a substantial number still have changes coming. The new standards are now in place.

Usually, if a school desires accreditation, the process will take two years—assuming the school passes the various hurdles.

A new Candidacy Partnership program establishes stable, ongoing, and helpful partnerships between AACSB and institutions working toward AACSB accreditation. "Candidacy" status signifies that the candidate institution is demonstrating reasonable progress toward attainment of accreditation. More than 100 schools are now in candidacy.

Keep in mind that normally you needn't concern yourself with whether the school you are considering is called a graduate school, a graduate division, an MBA program, or another master's business degree program. As long as the school is an autonomous degree-recommending unit that reports to the central administration, it is eligible to be considered for accreditation by AACSB.

Obviously, the fact that a school is accredited by AACSB should give you added confidence about the quality of its business program—a guarantee that a number of minimum standards have been met or surpassed. If you want complete details on the accrediting procedure, write to AACSB, 600 Emerson Road, Suite 300, St. Louis, MO 63141-6762. The Graduate Business Schools at a Glance chart and the individual business school entries in this book indicate which schools are accredited by AACSB.

One problem area that would-be graduate business students should be alert to is the fact that dozens of new MBA programs have sprung up to attract students and enhance a school's enrollments and finances. *Business Week* magazine reported that a number of schools now offering the MBA have seemed to relax academic standards to make their courses appealing to students who want a degree in the shortest amount of time and with the least amount of work. Chances are that in the next three years several schools that started MBA programs in the early 1980s will drop these programs because the market demand in some areas of the country is saturated or they get intense competition from schools offering distance learning courses. So a word of warning: It's safest to choose a graduate school that has been offering the MBA degree for at least 15 to 20 years.

The overall coordinating agency for accreditation programs is the Commission on Recognition of Postsecondary Accreditation (CORPA), the private sector oversight body for postsecondary accreditation.

If you are interested in a joint MBA or similar joint business program, here are the accrediting agencies of some of the fields in which you might be interested.

Health Services Administration

Accrediting Commission on Education for Health Services
 Administration
Patricia M. Sobczak
1911 North Fort Myer Drive
Suite 503
Arlington, VA 22209

Journalism

Accrediting Council on Education in Journalism and Mass
 Communications
c/o Susanne Shaw
School of Journalism
University of Kansas
Stauffer-Flint Hall
Lawrence, KS 66045

Law

American Bar Association
James P. White
Indiana University
550 West North Street
Indianapolis, IN 46202-3162

TEACHING METHODS

Most graduate schools of business organize their curricula around three basic elements: the core, the concentration, and electives. Core courses—usually finance, marketing, management, and accounting—provide an introduction to fundamental business concepts. The field of concentration is generally intended to provide advanced knowledge and specialized intensive preparation in an area of the student's major interest. Electives then offer a broad range of optional subjects.

However, there are wide differences in the ways various schools balance these three elements. Some schools offer a fixed curriculum with no field of specialization and no electives. Others either encourage or discourage specialization in areas like finance and accounting. Many schools spend a good deal of time on broad management courses that cut across many business disciplines. Some schools give students the opportunity to sample courses from a wide variety of areas in the business curriculum and sometimes even outside the business school; others don't. In a few schools, students can design programs that fit their personal interests or career goals.

There are constant shifts taking place in the schools and in their curricula, and this is being accelerated by the recent change in policies by AACSB several years ago. Harvard reduced both classroom time and reading materials by about 15 percent. The reduction was made after the faculty concluded that the school had been trying to deal with too many topics in too little time and in not enough depth. However, the workload still makes for a 65-hour week. At Stanford, professors may choose whatever methods suit their personal style and the materials they use. There has been a noticeable increase in team teaching and also bringing in professors from other disciplines, including history, religion, politics, and law.

There's also a shift to more production, operations management and productivity information systems, E-commerce, entrepreneurship, and international business courses, a reaction to business's growing need for managers who can run factories efficiently and compete with the growing inroads made by productivity-minded foreign manufacturers. MIT's Sloan School now offers majors in technology. Northeastern University has an MBA program specializing in high technology designed primarily for managers already in highly technical businesses. Rensselaer and Georgia Tech's DuPree School have an MBA concentration in the Management of Technology and Entrepreneurship. Quality control management is another area growing in popularity and is offered at a number of MBA schools such as IIT's Stuart School.

The international business course has become extremely popular in recent years and many new programs and courses have been developed to meet perceived needs. Courses in ethics and communications skills have also been added by many schools.

Business schools are now working on ways to involve business executives in the curriculum and teaching assignments. This has been aided by the appointments of some top former executives to dean positions at major business schools. This has been the case at Rice, Stanford, Fordham, Indiana, Boston, and other schools.

Teaching methods also vary from school to school, with each program emphasizing different elements. Harvard and the University of Virginia utilize the case method, which calls for the study and solution of problems actually faced by companies. Other schools, like Carnegie Mellon, are very involved in simulated "management games," where students work through business problems. The University of Chicago stresses economic and financial theory and recently became an innovator in business leadership programs, offering students courses that bridge the gap between classroom and marketplace. Some schools offer a great many seminars; others have lectures before large class groups. Many have role-playing; some utilize small group projects. Some schools are very practical in their approach. For example, the Keller Graduate School of Management has grown by accommodating students who desire a more practitioner-based program that schedules classes at times and locations convenient to working adult students. As for its instructors, Keller utilizes primarily business executives holding MBAs who have a commitment to excellence in teaching and who provide a practitioner's orientation to business management theories and concepts.

In a number of schools, students must undertake a substantial amount of research and writing; in others, oral presentations are emphasized. At one time, many graduate business schools required a thesis for an MBA. A recent survey shows that most schools do not require either a formal thesis or a written or oral examination for completion of the degree.

At the University of Buffalo (State University of New York), graduate business students coordinate their classroom efforts with the real business world by working on problems that involve local business concerns while earning credit for this experience. The Fuqua School (Duke) has a student consulting group that assists small North Carolina business firms as well as minority-owned businesses in the state.

At the University of Pennsylvania, students may do consulting projects for companies such as Continental Can Company, INA, and Chase Manhattan Bank. Many schools integrate course work with practical experience by encouraging students to work during summers or as part of the curriculum.

At Emory and the University of Texas, students work with managers of companies like Procter & Gamble, Motorola, and 3M in customer development work. General Electric and the University of Connecticut operate an E-commerce laboratory on the college's Stamford, Connecticut, campus.

In an effort to bring more realism into school work, a number of business schools offer special, innovative programs. At Texas Christian University, students taking the Seminar in Investments have total investment control of the university's Educational Investment Fund, which has over $1.5 million in portfolio assets. Similar programs are offered at the Kenan Flagler Business School (University of North Carolina), the University of Wisconsin at Madison, and Indiana University. At Florida Atlantic University, at least one course utilizes prominent businessmen and -women as lecturers. Loyola of Chicago has a Center for Family Business.

The Yale graduate school employs standard teaching methods but bases them on some rather unique concepts. Yale's plan is to educate leaders not only for corporations but for government, the military, and private foundations. The school wants to produce a versatile executive with a broad knowledge of how a variety of organizations operate. At the same time, students are trained in the full set of hard-edged management skills they might acquire in a more traditional MBA program. Columbia, the University of Texas, and others require every student to own a notebook computer.

How does a student decide what type of program will be best for him or her? There are no hard-and-fast guidelines, but most students will be served best by the more traditional program structure. A good solid grounding in business fundamentals is a must. The opportunity to concentrate on a special field of interest is also an advantage to the student. Most graduates will have to indicate

some preference for a particular field of specialty to prospective employers. They should, therefore, get enough of a taste of each of these areas while in graduate school so that they will (1) be sure they like a particular field, and (2) have taken enough courses in a specific field to step into a management training program or initial job without feeling they are in over their heads.

Regarding electives, their major advantage is in providing the opportunity to gain some insight into new fields—fields into which students might want to delve further when they enter the job world. Another advantage is that these electives can give the students a "rounding out" that may have ultimate value in their later careers.

As for teaching emphasis, if a student is practical-minded rather than theoretical, it is best for him or her to stay away from some of the business schools that place major stress on economic and business theory courses or the mathematical approach to business decision-making. Schools that offer practical courses like investment decision-making—utilizing actual investment funds—can be very advantageous. Likewise, taking courses that give you on-the-job training or consulting experience in the real business world can be very useful. Often, such experiences may provide the spark to put you on a future career path or give you the contacts that eventually result in a job offer.

A growing number of schools concentrate on developing the concept of teamwork among the MBA students. These schools believe that such courses will better prepare students for the job world. Keep in mind that MBA programs change with the times and with the needs of business and industry. In a number of schools, students work as a team on course work and projects and are graded as a team.

FULL TIME VERSUS PART TIME

The last time the federal government counted, for every two students attending full-time graduate business programs, there were three going to school part time. Indications are that the percentage of part-time students will probably increase in the next few years. The advent of distance learning courses will help cultivate this trend. The reason is simple: Many people decide to get their master's in business after they are already out in the job world. They don't want to give up their jobs to go to school full time. Also, a large number of men and women who would like to go to school full time simply can't afford to, and attending on a part-time basis is their only alternative.

As a result, many universities have MBA or other graduate business programs that make special provisions for and, in some cases, even cater to part-time students. Courses are given at night, in the early morning, on weekends, and over closed-circuit television by means of distance learning.

Students who do have the choice of going to school full time or part time should take a hard look at the pros and cons. Here are some advantages of being a part-time student:

- The costs will probably be much less.

- It indicates to your employer that you are ambitious, hard-working, and well motivated.

- If you are an employee and a part-time student, many companies will pay all or part of your tuition.

- You can often better comprehend the practical implications of the material being taught in the classroom if you hold a full-time job and go to school part time.

- You won't lose as much as two years' earnings or two years' work experience and promotion possibilities that you would if you attended school full time.

However, there are some substantial reasons for not opting for a part-time schedule:

- If you work full time, you might find yourself very tired and your attention span limited when you attend classes at night or on weekends.

- If you are working and raising a family, going to school puts additional pressure on your job, family, and marriage. Taking six hours of courses per semester can take a big slice of your time—as much as 18 hours a week.

- As a part-time student, you usually are unable to spend the same amount of preparation time for your classes, tests, and term papers that you could as a full-time student. Generally, you are expected to study two to three hours for each classroom hour. Also, you don't have the same access to library facilities, faculty members, or student advisers for research and discussion.

- You will have little chance to meet and spend time with your fellow students, to get to know them, or to make friendships, because you will generally arrive at school after work, with little time to spare, and will then leave as soon as class is over. It also means you rarely have time to participate in any extracurricular or social activities of the university, so you could miss what is generally called "the campus experience."

- It is difficult to build close relationships with your professors. You are usually under substantial time pressures, and many professors don't have office hours in the late afternoons or evenings, which are the times during which most part-time students can visit.

- There is also a question about the quality of many of the business programs geared to part-time students. A number of business programs that specialize in night school students, for example, rely heavily on part-time teachers. Others don't provide adequate library or computer resources at night. On the other hand, at a school like Fordham's Graduate School of Business, which offers primarily evening courses, but also has sizeable full-time and daytime programs, some 80 to 85 percent of all courses are taught by full-time faculty, and the program is accredited by AACSB. The same is true at many other MBA schools.

Some of the best business schools in the country do not offer evening or part-time courses. This list includes Harvard, Columbia, Dartmouth, and Stanford. It is also true that some leading corporations recruit for prospective employers solely among graduate business schools that have only full-time students.

On the other hand, some very fine graduate business schools do offer graduate business programs to part-time students, and their number is increasing. Two top business schools that offer programs geared to working students are New York University's Stern School of Business and the University of Chicago, which both offer prestigious day and evening programs. The schools treat the two programs as one, and offer the same faculty to night students as they do to full-time day students. The schools have only one set of admissions standards, and once admitted, students can transfer between day and evening classes without losing credit or continuity. Some Chicago professors even prefer the evening students because they feel they are more mature and dedicated.

More and more universities are providing not only evening courses but a variety of other schedules to accommodate part-time students. Some universities hold classes all day Friday or Saturday. The University of New Mexico, for example, offers a Friday-Saturday program. The Pace University Lubin Graduate School of Business at its New York City Midtown campus, as well as other schools, have an executive MBA program that meets on alternate Fridays and Saturdays. The University of Chicago has added a weekend program designed for busy executives, as have a number of other business schools.

Some programs even permit students to take graduate business courses right in their employers' offices or plants. Pace University offers a program that lets Pfizer employees complete an MBA program at Pfizer facilities in New York City. More and more such programs are cropping up because they save commuting time for working students. Also, employers sometimes allow such courses to begin on their premises in the late afternoon because it cuts down on the amount of time their employees have to spend attending school. Distance learning courses offer the opportunity to take courses at your office, home, or almost anywhere.

The University of South Carolina offers students a unique opportunity to earn the business master's via television while living and working almost anywhere in the state. This program is a joint effort of the university and the South Carolina Educational Television Network (SCETV) and is being emulated by other business schools. SCETV transmits lectures in each course to cities and towns throughout the state. Students simply go to the "classroom" nearest their home once or twice a week, where they watch lectures that are broadcast "live" from the system's parent classroom in Columbia, South Carolina. The students sit at desks equipped with talk-back capability with the instructor or fellow students. An average three-unit course consists of 30 hours of television instruction, usually in two-hour segments one night a week. In addition, four visits to the campus are required—on Saturdays, usually once each month—for computer work, counseling, and examinations.

Other schools set up satellite campuses to reach where students live and work. Illinois Institute of Technology, for example, opened minicenters in the Chicago suburbs of Wheaton and Schaumburg. The programs in Wheaton reach engineers who want to get their MBAs at nearby companies.

DISTANCE LEARNING

Probably the most important development taking place in graduate business schools is the trend toward establishing distance learning programs. Distance learning utilizes many techniques and equipment such as radio, TV, computers, CDs, video, chat rooms, and so on to bring courses to students no matter where they are—at home, in the office, and across continents.

Today, an estimated 30 to 50% of graduate business schools are offering such courses and the trend is gaining momentum each month. Distance learning opens the door for thousands of students to get their MBAs, usually at their convenience and in many cases having to be on the campus for only a few days or weeks, or not at all.

Today, at least 70 schools, some of them AACSB-accredited, offer an MBA in their distance learning program. In addition, there are a growing number of new schools established for the major purpose of providing distance learning, for example, Jones International University, Kaplan University, and Cardean University. Cardean was created by a group of business schools—Chicago, Stanford, Carnegie Mellon, and Columbia. They are mainly for-profit institutions without campuses.

The students enrolled in these courses to date tend to be in their thirties and forties and are generally middle management. They tend to be self-disciplined, ambitious, serious, and well motivated. They are taking these courses because it is more convenient than going to a campus and because they can take the course material usually on a very flexible schedule and don't have to commit to given days, nights, or weekends. These courses usually cost more than the standard courses, but the offset is that in most cases their companies pay part or all of the cost.

Are students who get their MBAs through distance learning any better or worse than those who don't? So far, the research has been minimal, but to date some schools report that they seem to be on par. However, in some cases, the dropout rate of distance learning students seems to be higher than regular part-time students.

While there are a number of advantages for students through distance learning, there are a number of obvious drawbacks. A student does not have a "campus experience," nor does he usually have much or any contact with fellow students and professors. While there are chat rooms and other means of getting involved with students and teachers, it is not comparable to being in a classroom.

It is also not clear how corporate recruiters will regard the distance learning MBA. Will they regard it as the equivalent of a traditional MBA and hire accordingly? Only time will tell.

Distance learning also poses a number of concerns for graduate business schools. Will they pay extra, and perhaps premiums, to professors who develop and teach such courses? Do the professors who develop such courses own the courses or does the college? Will the college utilize tapes and material of prestigious professors at other colleges or utilize their own faculty exclusively? Can smaller business colleges survive the threat of major business schools offering their degrees through distance learning?

Clearly there are many concerns and problems as well as opportunities, but it seems obvious that distance learning will change the face of graduate business education in the years to come.

HOW LONG DOES IT TAKE?

While many graduate business degree programs require two academic years if pursued on a full-time basis, some programs can run as short as one year if the student has had substantial undergraduate work in business. At Babson, you can earn your degree in one year. Some schools allow advanced standing on the basis of undergraduate courses, but usually these decisions are made only upon an individual review of the student's records. To qualify for advanced standing, the best bet is to have an undergraduate degree in business administration and to get the master's degree from the same university.

A substantial number of graduate business schools allow students to accelerate their studies by offering year-round programs and by permitting them to enter school in the spring and summer as well as in the fall. Pace offers four terms a year, and a student can start in any term. The Columbia Graduate School of Business offers three terms a year and a student can start in any term. But at many graduate schools, such as Carnegie Mellon and Cornell, students may begin only in the fall. So, if you are interested in getting your master's degree in the shortest possible time, concentrate on those schools that offer year-round courses and permit you to enter during any term.

If you are a part-time student, it is important to check admissions policies carefully, because you probably will want to earn your degree in the shortest time, and you may want to study all year round. It is also important to see what sequences of courses and electives are offered each semester so you don't have to wait out a semester until a course you need is given.

Most part-time programs run four years, but this, too, varies considerably. If you plan to go part-time, figure that at most you can take two courses per semester. Going to school three semesters per year, you could take 18 semester hours per year. If the degree requirement is 48 hours, you could finish in two and two-third years' time. On the other hand, if you need 60 hours for your degree, it will take five years at six hours a semester, two semesters a year, and three and one-third years if you go three semesters a year. Table 1 gives you some guidelines concerning how long it will take you to finish your program on a part-time basis.

FIELDS OF SPECIALIZATION

At those schools where students can specialize in one or more areas of business, the most popular fields are accounting, finance, marketing, and management. A study by Korn/Ferry International and The Anderson School at UCLA surveyed business executives several years ago to find out what specialities they thought were the fastest route to the top. Some 25 percent of the respondents felt that the financial/accounting route was the best way to get to the top; 35 percent said that marketing/sales was the best; 23 percent said general management; 7 percent said professional/technical; and 6 percent indicated that production/manufacturing was the best route. Currently the very popular areas are international business, E-commerce, and entrepreneurship.

These trends often are a reflection of what employers are looking for in graduates and what fields offer the highest starting pay.

TABLE 1
HOW LONG IT CAN TAKE YOU TO EARN YOUR MASTER'S IN BUSINESS AS A PART-TIME STUDENT

SEMESTER HOURS REQUIRED FOR DEGREE	TWO COURSES PER TERM, THREE TERMS A YEAR	TWO COURSES PER SEMESTER, TWO SEMESTERS A YEAR	ONE COURSE PER TERM, THREE TERMS A YEAR	ONE COURSE PER SEMESTER, TWO SEMESTERS A YEAR
60	3⅓ years	5 years	6⅔ years	10 years
48	2⅔ years	4 years	5⅓ years	8 years
36	2 years	3 years	4 years	6 years
30	1⅔ years	2½ years	3⅓ years	5 years

For example, banks and insurance companies are usually interested in students who concentrate on finance, whereas accounting firms are interested in accounting and finance majors, and retail firms look for marketing majors.

Keep in mind that these patterns always tend to be in a state of flux. Don't jump into a major field just because it is "hot" for the time being. You are better off picking a field that you like and for which you feel you have special aptitude and talent.

SCHOOL RANKINGS

As pointed out earlier, most graduate business candidates are part-time students who mainly choose their graduate business schools on the basis of accessibility to where they live and work, courses offered, and the reputation of the institution. Accessibility may become less of a factor as distance learning courses become more widespread.

For most full-time students, other key criteria include the cost of attending and the length of time it will take to get the degree. The full-time student with average grades and test scores will find many schools that meet his or her needs and must simply figure out what criteria to weigh the heaviest. Those students who want to attend full time, who have excellent grades, and to whom the location and cost of attending graduate business school are not serious problems really have a difficult decision in selecting a school. Most students in this situation opt for the best business school.

This brings us to the question of which is the best graduate business school in the country and which schools are the runners-up. The quick answer is that no one can be sure of just which school is the "best," but we can determine fairly well a number of schools that are considered among the best. Actually, there are about 20 to 30 graduate business schools that are considered to be "top drawer" schools and that have the reputation of being national business schools. By "national," we mean that the stu-

dent enrollment is drawn from a very wide geographic area and that major companies from all over the country recruit on their campuses.

With regard to ranking these schools, there are countless arguments about which one is best. In fact, every time a ranking study is made it triggers off dozens of letters from the schools, their graduates, and faculty, all complaining that the particular study and its results are invalid. As a result, while there have been a number of studies done in recent years attempting to rank business schools, there have been serious reservations about the results of a number of those studies. Some of the ratings are based on rather unscientific samplings and highly subjective judgments. For many years, Harvard was considered the best. It has an outstanding faculty, and the job history of Harvard business school graduates has been spectacular.

Very interesting studies of the graduate business schools that have turned out the largest number of successful top executives are done by Standard & Poor's Compmark Data Services. The studies were made by analyzing the files of *Poor's Register,* which contains data on over 70,000 executives representing more than 55,000 of the nation's leading corporations. The executives were either chairmen, presidents, vice presidents, or directors of companies.

Previous studies had been done in 1998, 1996, 1994, 1992, 1990, 1987, 1985, 1982, 1980, and 1976. In the 2000 study, results indicated that more than 20,000 of the country's leading business executives held graduate-level degrees.

Since the first full survey, when the top 12 schools were ranked according to the number of graduates who were top business executives, only one college has entered the top 12 list and only one has dropped from it. Over the years, Harvard, New York University, and Columbia continue to dominate the results. Indications are that through the sheer numbers of graduates these three schools produce, they will continue to dominate.

TABLE 2
COMPARATIVE RESULTS OF S&P's COLLEGE/EXECUTIVE SURVEY
2000, 1998, 1996, 1994, 1992

Number of Executive Alumni with Graduate Degrees

2000		1998		1996		1994		1992	
1. Harvard	2301	1. Harvard	2315	1. Harvard	2470	1. Harvard	2828	1. Harvard	3061
2. NYU	981	2. NYU	979	2. NYU	1045	2. NYU	1262	2. NYU	1316
3. Columbia	923	3. Columbia	924	3. Columbia	945	3. Columbia	1077	3. Columbia	1125
4. U. Penn.	846	4. U. Penn	777	4. U. Penn	782	4. U. Penn	849	4. U. Penn	857
5. U. Chicago	707	5. U. Chicago	697	5. U. Chicago	682	5. U. Chicago	758	5. U. Michigan	764
6. Stanford	617	6. U. Michigan	610	6. U. Michigan	619	6. U. Michigan	709	6. U. Chicago	747
7. Northwestern	615	7. Northwestern	573	7. Northwestern	558	7. Northwestern	595	7. Northwestern	622
8. U. California	597	8. U. California	536	8. U. California	521	8. U. California	585	8. Stanford	588
9. U. Michigan	591	9. Stanford	531	9. Stanford	496	9. Stanford	523	9. U. California	572
10. U. Wisconsin	483	10. U. Wisconsin	465	10. U. Wisconsin	464	10. U. Wisconsin	521	10. U. Wisconsin	534
11. MIT	429	11. MIT	398	11. MIT	425	11. Rutgers	486	11. MIT	513
12. Rutgers	361	12. Rutgers	389	12. Rutgers	395	12. MIT	479	12. Rutgers	502

Figures compiled by Standard & Poor's Register of Corporations, Directors and Executives and Compmark Data Services, a division of Standard & Poor's Corp., 2000. Reprinted with permission.

The 2000 study found that Harvard has more corporate executives as alumni than do the next two top graduate business schools combined. Second and third place went to New York University and Columbia University. The schools are ranked by the number of their executive alumni listed in *Poor's Register.* While the survey did not specify that the graduate degree was a business degree, the presumption is that this is the predominant degree by a wide margin.

The results of the survey are shown in Table 2.

Just which is the best business school? This is a question that continually comes up but is very difficult to answer. There is no one universally accepted rating standard, but the results of several surveys seem to indicate that Harvard, Chicago, Stanford, University of Pennsylvania, and Northwestern are at the very top of the heap.

In fact the ratings of graduate business schools in recent years by *Business Week* magazine and *U.S. News & World Report* have resulted in a great deal of nail biting by the deans of many business schools. It is a fact that the ratings by those publications—particularly the *Business Week* rankings—have resulted in a substantial increase in applications to the business schools that have ranked high on the lists. These ratings have also put pressure on the administration of a substantial number of business schools to improve their ratings. This has resulted in some changes in business school curriculums, and also in extensive communications programs to the business world and prospective students touting the advantages of the various schools. A number of graduate business schools have hired public relations firms, at fees in excess of $100,000 a year, to help tell their stories and improve their image.

Each of the magazines uses different criteria and sampling methods to rate business schools.

Table 3 lists the top 10 graduate business schools as ranked by *Business Week* magazine, appearing in the October 2, 2000 issue of the magazine.

Table 4 lists the top 10 graduate business schools according to *U.S. News & World Report* magazine, which appeared in the April 9, 2001 issue of the magazine.

The first point regarding ratings is that there are many ways to rank schools, and it is hard to say which is the best way. The second point is that if you want to go to one of the best schools, you will find the names of the same schools appearing in almost any list of the top 20, but they don't always rank the same way in each survey.

A third point is that the major schools are in fierce competition for bright students and believe that the various surveys ranking the schools can influence students' choices. Many graduate schools wish that such ranking surveys would disappear, but since they won't, the schools are anxious to make sure they show up well on such rankings.

Once you get beyond the top national schools, you have about 100 regional schools that draw students mainly from the regional areas. The remaining schools, which total more than 600, usually draw on students from a more limited geographic area.

One other key fact to consider that will have a great impact on these schools' future ratings and program quality are their current development efforts. Many schools have recently received or plan to obtain substantial new funds to help them recruit outstanding faculty and provide improved facilities and new programs. Such funds include $50 million to the University of Texas, $60 million to the University of Virginia, $40 million to Houston University, $25 million to Fairfield University, and $35 million to Notre Dame.

TABLE 3
TOP 10 BUSINESS SCHOOLS AS RANKED BY
BUSINESS WEEK **MAGAZINE**

1. University of Pennsylvania (Wharton)
2. Northwestern University (Kellogg)
3. Harvard University
4. MIT (Sloan)
5. Duke University (Fuqua)
6. University of Michigan
7. Columbia University
8. Cornell University (Johnson)
9. University of Virginia (Darden)
10. University of Chicago

From *Business Week* magazine, October 2, 2000.

TABLE 4
TOP 10 BUSINESS SCHOOLS AS RANKED BY
U.S. NEWS & WORLD REPORT **MAGAZINE**

1. Stanford University
2. Harvard University
3. Northwestern University (Kellogg)
4. University of Pennsylvania (Wharton)
5. MIT (Sloan)
6. Columbia University
7. University of California–Berkeley (Haas)
8. Duke University (Fuqua)
9. University of Chicago
10. University of Michigan

From *U.S. News & World Report* magazine, April 9, 2001.

SUITABILITY OF UNDERGRADUATE BUSINESS MAJORS VERSUS UNDERGRADUATE NONBUSINESS MAJORS

Most schools do not insist that those wanting to enroll in graduate business programs must have majored in business as undergraduates. In fact, one recent trend among those entering graduate business schools is to major in engineering. Currently, the combination of an undergraduate engineering degree plus an MBA is highly prized by many companies. However, if you have not had a sizable number of undergraduate business courses, you may have to attend graduate school longer than the student with undergraduate business training. The major disadvantage for nonbusiness majors is that they may be asked to take a number of prerequisite courses before commencing the actual master's program. In some cases, deficiencies in mathematics or economics might have to be remedied before admittance is possible as a regular student.

At some graduate schools, there are distinct disadvantages for those who have not taken a great number of undergraduate business courses. On the other hand, at Carnegie Mellon and other schools that put special emphasis on quantitative courses, mathematics, and computer skills, it is felt that students with undergraduate business courses do not have the most desirable backgrounds. You can easily find out whether undergraduate business courses are an important consideration to a particular graduate business school by studying the entry on the school in this book.

COSTS: STATE VERSUS PRIVATE

One important consideration if you are on a budget is the fact that tuition at city and state universities is usually much lower than that at most private universities. The difference can be as much as $20,000 a year, so for a two-year graduate program you could save as much as $40,000 by going to the business school of a state university in your own state rather than attending a private university. Also, keep in mind that even if you go to a state university as a non-state resident, the tuition costs will probably be less than those of a good private university. There are a number of state universities with excellent graduate schools of business, including the University of Michigan/Ann Arbor, the University of Virginia, Georgia Tech, the University of California/Berkeley and Los Angeles, Purdue University (Krannert), the University of Texas at Austin, the University of Illinois, Indiana University, and a number of others.

Your Admission Chances

Your chances of being admitted depend primarily on your undergraduate grade-point average (GPA) and on your GMAT score (if the graduate school requires a GMAT score). Other factors enter into the admissions decision, but these two are of prime importance. In some cases, there is an advantage if you have work or military experience. If you are a woman or a member of a minority, this, too, may increase your chances of gaining admission. You are also at an advantage if you are a resident applying to a graduate business school in your home state.

AS AN IMMEDIATE COLLEGE GRADUATE

Here you are staking your chances almost exclusively on your undergraduate record and your GMAT test score. If you want to know how you rate, compare your GMAT score with the average score listed in the individual entry sections of this book. Generally speaking, a growing number of schools are using the AACSB-recommended method of combining GPA with GMAT score. The formula is to take your overall undergraduate GPA, multiply it by 200, and then add the GMAT score. Or, you can take your upper-division GPA, multiply it by 200, and add the GMAT score. In any case, the AACSB recommends that the graduate school only accept students who have a minimum of 950 if they use the overall GPA, or 1000 if they use the upper-division GPA. (See the earlier section titled, "Accreditation.") If you don't meet these minimums, you will have a difficult time getting into an AACSB-accredited school. However, you will find a substantial number of non-AACSB-accredited schools that will accept students with C averages and fairly low GMAT scores.

AS A COLLEGE GRADUATE WITH WORK EXPERIENCE

If you have your undergraduate degree and several years of business or military experience, you will find that at many schools you will have an edge over candidates fresh out of college. A growing number of graduate schools prefer students who have full-time business experience of two to five years. This work experience can demonstrate job proficiency and interest in business, and students with such experience are often more serious and can relate class work better with the real business world. At Stanford, nearly 100 percent of the entering students had at least two years of full-time work experience before coming to Stanford. At Harvard, most entering students have two or more years of work experience. At Wharton, the average student has four years of work experience. At the University of Texas at Austin, work experience is assuming increased importance in the admissions practice. The trend is for MBA students to have an increasing amount of work experience before starting their MBA program.

There are some disadvantages to going back to school full-time after an interruption of several years, but most of them are personal. Often, you make a greater financial sacrifice by going back to college once you have been working in the business world. Also, relearning study habits and the knack of taking tests might be difficult.

AS A MINORITY GROUP MEMBER

If you are a member of a minority group, your chances of getting into a graduate school of business are better now than at almost any point in the past. Many graduate schools are spending considerable effort to increase their representation of African-Americans, Native Americans, Hispanics, Asian-Americans, and other minority groups.

In 2000, the percentage of ethnic minorities, including Hispanics, Orientals, Native Americans, and African-Americans, was estimated at more than 10 percent of all MBA students. The enrollment of African-American students is estimated to be around the 7 percent level and has stayed around that level for several years.

Several organizations are trying to reverse this trend. The National Black MBA Association is developing a series of programs designed to attract minority MBA students. Coca-Cola, General Motors, Ford, Citicorp, and others have signed up as partners of the National Black MBA Association in a drive to get more African-Americans enrolled in MBA programs. Michigan and MIT have the highest percentage of minority students among the top 10 business schools according to a recent survey.

Some of the recruitment programs are done under special consortium arrangements, with funding provided by major non-profit foundations. The Consortium of Graduate Study in Management recruits minority students, using funds from foundations and businesses. Consortium schools include the Universities of Southern California, Wisconsin, Rochester, Michigan, North Carolina, Texas (Austin), Virginia, and California (Berkeley); Indiana and Washington (St. Louis) Universities; and New York University's Stern School of Business. Consortium fellowships provide free tuition. For more information, write Consortium for Graduate Study in Management, 200 South Hanley, Suite 1102, St. Louis, MO 63105-3415. More than 2,600 students have graduated using this program.

AS A WOMAN

The number of women attending graduate business schools has been on the increase for quite a few years now, and at many schools they comprise over 35 percent of the student body. In 2000 it was estimated that about 39 percent of all MBA students were women. At the Stern School at NYU for the class of 2001, 39 percent of the students are women. Many graduate business schools are making an effort to increase the enrollment of women students. This is in keeping with the revolution in attitudes towards women executives that is taking place in American business. In contrast to the situation only 10 to 15 years ago, women executives have become well accepted by top executives in most major corporations. In most large companies, top executives are focusing on performance whether they are assessing a man or a woman executive.

The percentage is very high, of course, at Simmons College Graduate School of Management in Boston, a predominantly women's school that established the first graduate management program for women in 1974. Simmons' program may be completed in 12 months of intensive full-time study or in two or three years of part-time enrollment. In addition to course work comparable to that at other business schools, Simmons offers special courses in the behavioral area that are particularly useful to women who aspire to be managers. Case studies feature women managers and emphasis is on helping prepare women students to play a leadership role in business. Also, entering students average 32 years old and have 10 years of work experience.

The present effort that graduate business schools are making to recruit women may include special financial aid funds and placement services. Other sources women might want to check for aid or programs are the Business and Professional Women's Foundation, 2012 Massachusetts Avenue, N.W., Washington, DC 20036 (for both scholarships and loan programs), and local chapters of the American Association of University Women (AAUW).

In its October 1998 issue, *Working Women* magazine did a survey to determine the most woman-friendly graduate business schools. The top 10 were: Columbia, University of Michigan, University of California at Berkeley, Northwestern (Kellogg School), University of Virginia, Stanford, Duke, University of North Carolina (Kenan-Flagler School), Ohio State University, and University of Pennsylvania (Wharton).

While there has been an increase of women in the MBA program, there still seem to be some problems concerning how women MBAs fare once they go into the job world. The woman MBA at the entry level usually feels quite welcome in her first job. After three or five years she may get somewhat frustrated and feels that her hard work and talent are not being recognized in pay and promotion the way her male colleagues' work and talent are.

So, while the influx of women MBAs has helped make a great deal of progress in increasing the position of women in the business world, there are still sizable roadblocks that have to be overcome.

AS AN INTERNATIONAL STUDENT

One major development in recent years is the heavy influx of foreign students to American graduate business schools. They come mainly from Europe and the Far East—Japan, China, South Korea, India, Malaysia, and Taiwan. The reasons are many. In the Far East, there are few graduate business schools and none with the high reputation of the American schools. A degree in the United States is a bargain for many foreign students. Many students go to school in the United States and then return to top posts in their native countries armed with the prestigious American MBA degree. Others are interested in learning American business techniques and also in getting a better sense of American thinking. More than one third of the applications to top business schools are filed by foreign students and they comprise more than 10 percent of the student body at graduate business schools.

As a result, the number of foreign students as a percentage of total MBA enrollments is growing. At New York University (Stern), about 33 percent of the students are foreign; at Stanford, 31 per-

cent; at UCLA, 19 percent; at Yale, 33 percent; at the University of Chicago, 32 percent; at Northwestern (Kellogg), 25 percent.

An increasing number of European and Latin American students are also attending. A number of years ago, Harvard admitted the first Russian MBA students. After graduation, they will fulfill a five-year commitment to work in their home country.

Some Japanese firms make it especially attractive for their employees to study at American business schools. In many cases, these Japanese firms pay tuition and all school expenses, provide special living allowances, and pay their employees' salaries while they are studying in the United States. They may also permit their employees' families to join them in the United States at company expense.

International students are generally expected to meet the same admission standards as those set for everyone else. One major concern business schools have regarding international students is their proficiency in English. Usually the school's admissions committee will want to see evidence that a student can understand rapidly spoken idiomatic English, participate in class discussions, and be able to write reports and other required materials.

Because of this concern, most business schools require international students whose university training was not conducted in English to demonstrate their proficiency through the Test of English as a Foreign Language (TOEFL). Barron's *How to Prepare for the TOEFL* provides special help to those who plan to take the TOEFL exam. International students should also keep in mind that the Graduate Management Admission Test (GMAT) is given only in English. The test may not be taken more than once a month.

One problem schools have had in evaluating the applications of international students is determining the quality and caliber of their undergraduate work. Their transcripts are usually written in a foreign language, and course titles, contents, and the semester credit systems at foreign universities can be totally different from those of American schools. This is one reason why it is important for international students to submit their applications to business schools at least one year in advance.

Another way admissions policies toward international students differ from those accorded American students is that business schools often require them to finish *all* their undergraduate academic work before considering them for admission.

It would be advisable for international students to determine well in advance just how much special assistance they can get from the business schools in which they are interested. Some schools have special advisers and programs for international students; others have no special programs, and international students are left to more or less shift for themselves. Typical of the school that offers special services to international students is the University of Michigan. Its International Center helps foreign students with housing, immigration problems, and personal adjustment. Students should also keep in mind that most business schools won't make financial aid available to them during their first year of graduate school. However, there are some outstanding overseas MBA schools, and both foreign and American students are now finding these schools increasingly attractive. In fact, the AACSB now accredits seven schools in Canada, two in Mexico, six in Europe, and three in Asia.

International students who want more specific information on graduate study opportunities as well as on how to cope with special problems they will face at American schools should write or visit the U.S. Information Service educational advising center(s) in their home countries. International students may get useful information from the Institute of International Education, 809 United Nations Plaza, New York, NY 10017. The Institute cannot provide research assistance by mail or phone, but offers several books

that may be purchased from the address above, including *English Language and Orientation Programs in the United States* ($42.95) and *Funding for U.S. Study: A Guide for Foreign Nationals* ($39.98).

THE LARGEST ENROLLMENTS

TABLE 5

Largest Master's Degree Programs by Enrollment (Full Time)

College	Enrollment
1. University of Phoenix	6,737
2. Webster University	1,525
3. Brigham Young University	604
4. University of Florida	412
5. Keller Graduate School of Management	411
6. Texas A&M University	395
7. George Washington University	379
8. University of Houston (Clear Lake)	370
9. Troy State University	365
10. Georgia State University	323
11. University of Illinois (Urbana-Champaign)	254
12. University of Denver	246

AACSB 1999–2000 Survey.

TABLE 6

Largest Business Schools by Enrollment (Full Time)

College	Enrollment
1. University of Pennsylvania	1,691
2. Columbia University	1,578
3. Thunderbird: The American Graduate School of International Management	1,486
4. Harvard University	1,452
5. Pepperdine University	1,133
6. University of Chicago	1,124
7. University of Michigan	1,026
8. University of Texas (Austin)	778
9. Stanford University	723
10. MIT (Sloan)	713

AACSB 1999–2000 Survey. Only AACSB-accredited schools listed.

TABLE 7

Largest Business Schools
by Enrollment
(Part Time)

College	Enrollment
1. DePaul University	2,176
2. University of Chicago	1,719
3. Saint Joseph's University	1,528
4. Wayne State University	1,509
5. Fordham University	1,223
6. Georgia State University	1,222
7. Rutgers University	1,114
8. University of Michigan	1,048
9. Pace University	1,004
10. University of Connecticut	917

AACSB 1999–2000 Survey. Only AACSB-accredited schools listed.

The Application Procedure

Admission Requirements

Applications for admission to graduate business schools continue to be impressive. This past year, more than 175,000 potential MBA students took the GMAT. Currently it is estimated that for every opening in a quality graduate business school there are almost two applicants, and at some of the more prestigious schools such as Harvard, Stanford, Chicago, and Michigan, there are 10 or more applicants for each available opening.

- Basically, there are four requirements for admission to a graduate school of business:

- A bachelor's degree from a recognized educational institution.

- An acceptable test score on the Graduate Management Admission Test (GMAT).

- An academic standing that meets the school's criteria. This can range from the upper half of your undergraduate class to the top 10 percent, depending on the graduate school to which you apply. Some schools also have specific grade-point averages they require as a minimum.

- Most international students must have an acceptable score on the Test of English as a Foreign Language (TOEFL).

While not all colleges will supply specific information on the minimum GMAT scores required, most will provide average scores and ranges of scores from their last admissions group. These figures are shown in the individual school entries in this book.

The same is true of your undergraduate grades. Many graduate schools have fixed ideas of the minimum grade-point average (GPA) they will accept—or the minimum class standing. Again, this may not be indicated in the college catalogs, but admission officials will supply this information if you speak with them. Schools tend to avoid putting such information in print because there are a great many intangibles they consider when looking at an applicant's record. For example, a B average from Princeton will probably carry more weight with an admissions committee than a B+ from a second-rate university. The committee also looks at more than grades. They take note of the courses and course load you took to see if you had a "heavy" or "light" load, and easy or difficult courses. They will also look at the trend of your grades. Did you start as a C student and wind up an A student by the time you graduated? Or, did you start as a B student and stay a B student for four years? They may look at your grades in your major field and see how long it has been since you finished your college work.

Most graduate business schools do not require undergraduate courses in business administration or other specific fields and will consider applicants who have majored in a wide range of fields. Some business schools, however, may require college mathematics, calculus, and statistics, and if you did not take such courses, you may have to take them before being fully admitted to the graduate school. Other schools may require some minimal business or economics undergraduate courses. Here again you may be admitted without them but will have to make up this deficiency before you are classified as a regular student.

Most admissions committees look with favor upon applicants who have a good grounding in an experimental science or in psychology. They also are interested to see if an applicant has the ability to speak and write English well. A substantial number of schools, like Harvard, emphasize work experience before beginning a graduate business program. In almost every case, work experience is given substantial consideration in evaluating candidates.

In many schools, special admissions criteria are used in evaluating applicants from minority groups or from distant countries (colleges often like to publicize the fact that their student body comes from so many different states and countries). On the other hand, state university business schools favor state residents, and private schools may look favorably at relatives of alumni.

Keep in mind that there may be substantial differences in admissions standards within the same business school depending on the type of program. Admission standards for part-time students may be different from those for full-time students. The requirements for a specialized degree program, say an MBA with a specialty in taxation, may be more or less stringent than the regular MBA program at the same school, depending on whether the school is trying to increase or hold down enrollments.

Also, remember that admissions policies are formulated by different groups at the various universities, and this can mean sizable variations. Generally, the key people involved in admissions decisions are the faculty committee, dean, director of admissions, and a governing board or central graduate school advisory board. The admissions officer is usually the person responsible for administering and carrying out the admissions policies.

To apply to a graduate school, there are several documents you must usually submit. These include:

- The completed application form.

- One or more transcripts of your undergraduate courses and grades. Grades for any course in progress at the time the admissions decision is made must usually be reported to the school prior to enrollment. However, unless you completely fail your final semester, chances are that once you are admitted, the business school won't reverse that decision.

- Letters of recommendation.

- GMAT score.

- Rank in class.

- Application fee.

Advanced Standing and Transfer

If you feel there is a chance you might be eligible for advanced standing for courses taken at undergraduate or graduate school or for work experience, apply for it. The worst that can happen is that you don't get it. Most university catalogs will tell you whether or not transfer credit is accepted. Keep in mind that regulations vary considerably between one school and another. For example, at the Kenan Flagler Business School (University of North Carolina) there is no waiver of program requirements on the basis of undergraduate work. At the University of Michigan, students may waive some required courses by passing a placement exam and then can take an elective course in its place. At the University of Chicago, transfer credits can't reduce the required number of hours, but students are able to take more electives.

At Boston University, students may accelerate their programs by transferring graduate credit from other accredited schools and having course requirements waived. At Columbia, advanced standing toward the MBA is awarded only to those students who are enrolled in a recognized Columbia University joint degree program. The Illinois Institute of Technology (IIT) will waive up to three courses for students who took undergraduate courses in equivalent areas. At the University of Southern California, students can transfer a maximum of four units of graduate work at the A or B level, but only from approved graduate schools.

The point is that if you have done graduate work already or have had a heavy concentration of business administration and economics courses as an undergraduate, it is worthwhile to try to get credit for these courses.

When to Apply

Most school catalogs indicate the deadline for admission applications. Usually it is anywhere from March 1 to August 1 (and most likely before June 1) for those planning to enter graduate school in the fall. However, some admissions officers will advise that applying as much as a year in advance can be advantageous. This is particularly true for international students. And, if you intend to apply for financial aid or for some type of assistantship or scholarship, applying one year in advance may also be to your advantage. In addition, by applying early you can sometimes avoid the complicated and embarrassing negotiations of delaying reply dates to one graduate school while you are waiting to hear about admission to another school.

It is important to keep in mind that it takes time for your credentials and other materials to reach the various schools for their evaluation. You will also need to plan ahead to prepare for and take the GMAT examination that most business schools require.

How to Help Your Chances of Being Admitted

Once you are a college senior and have taken your GMAT, you can't do much to alter your academic standing or your test scores. But that doesn't mean your application has to stand or fall simply on the basis of these statistics. The way you fill out your application and handle items such as letters of recommendation and personal interviews can be very important, particularly if you are a borderline admissions case.

THE APPLICATION FORM

Regardless of what the instructions say about it being permissible to fill out the form in ink, don't do it. Type it or have a professional type it. One good tip is to make a copy of the application form or get two application forms and use one as your rough draft. A neatly typed, good-looking application form can be a plus in admissions. More than 15 percent of the applications in 2000 are believed to have been computer generated.

Make sure you respond to all the questions. Your grammar and punctuation should be impeccable. If you are a poor speller or grammarian, have someone who is good at these skills look over your application before it is typed. If you have to write an essay, make sure it is your best effort. You may have to rewrite it several times before it is ready to be typed. Again, it pays to show the essay to friends, relatives, or anyone who has an eye for good, clear writing. There are now computer software programs available that can cut down on the time required if you are submitting multiple applications.

Where you list extracurricular activities on the application, be sure to put your best foot forward. The admissions committee wants to know whether you are well-rounded, versatile, a self-starter, or an innovator. List those activities that show you have some or all of these traits. Unique activities always catch the eye. Are you a tournament bridge player, a sky diver, an astronomer, or a commodities speculator? If so, be sure to mention it.

Work experience does count heavily, so list your previous jobs and responsibilities carefully. The admissions committee looks at this item closely to see if you are a hard worker, are willing to assume responsibility, and have a record of job achievements. The student who went to college and held a job simultaneously is often given positive consideration. If you have had full-time work experience, play it up. If you have done only part-time work, list your jobs in a way that indicates the value of such experience.

If the school wants you to write one or more essays, try to be creative but not cute. Show them by the way you write your essay that you are keenly interested in getting an MBA, giving your reason, and that you believe you have the attributes to be successful in the business world. It is recommended that you spend five to ten hours on your application, particularly your essays.

LETTERS OF RECOMMENDATION

Letters of recommendation can be important, so you should give considerable attention to deciding whom to list as references. Consider those people you know who will give the time and attention necessary in writing a reference or in filling out the recommendation form the school sends them. Also, choose people who you feel will complete the recommendations by the deadline dates, so their letters will be reviewed.

You probably have a wide range of references to choose from—professors, business acquaintances, family friends, and alumni of the business school. Don't bother to list millionaires, ministers, congressmen, or judges as references unless you are sure they will write a favorable and individualized reference for you. You don't want mediocre or routine letters of recommendation. You don't want letters that say what a great athlete or social charmer you are. You do want letters that say you have the character, talent, and intelligence to do well at business school and in the business world.

If you are out of ideas about whom to list as a reference, ask the professor who gave you your highest grades. Another approach is to look to the younger professors; some of the older ones may be tired of writing recommendations and their letters may look tired, too. Generally, avoid the most popular professors; they may be swamped.

Before you finally decide on whom to list as references, call or write and ask them if they will agree to help you. At the same time, it might be a good idea to suggest to these persons that you would be pleased to send them some material on the criteria the school uses in screening students, as well as a summary sketch of your background and accomplishments. This way, you will be providing your references with material they can use in their letters.

If a reference asks that you write the first draft of the letter that he or she will then edit, jump at the chance. Also, keep in mind that if you are writing summaries for three different references, give each of them some unique and different material. This will prevent their reference letters from commenting on almost identical traits using the same illustrations.

Obviously, collecting the right references and getting them to write recommendations that are super takes a lot of work, but if you want to be a success in the business world, this is the kind of project you'll be engaged in continuously. So, you might as well start now.

Is it worthwhile to ask business acquaintances and others to try to "pull some strings" to help get you into a good business school? In answering this question, you have to be guided by some knowledge of the particular graduate school involved and also by common sense. For example, if you are asked to give three recommendations and you give three, but then you ask a dozen people to write letters to the college urging that they admit you, you are asking for trouble because you have applied overkill. On the other hand, it is usually good if one or two prominent business people or others write unsolicited letters to the admissions committee urging your admission. Keep in mind that if the director of admissions or dean thinks that you and your family are applying unusual pressure to gain admittance, it might trigger a negative reaction and work to your disadvantage.

The people who probably carry the most weight with admissions groups are members of the business school's faculty, members of the university's faculty, prominent alumni of the business school, and prominent businessmen or -women. If you can't use any of these people as references but you do have a chance to contact them, indicate that you are very much interested in being admitted to the specific business school. These professors and businesspeople are smart enough to know that you have given them this information with the hope that they can be helpful. If they want to help they will, but if they don't want to for one reason or another, your informal request hasn't put them under any pressure.

Should You Visit the Campus?

By all means visit the schools you are interested in if you have the time and can afford the trip. Nothing takes the place of a personal visit. It gives you a feel for the school and its environment and the personality of the students, and enables you to meet school officials and ask them questions. If you can arrange an interview and you do well in interview situations, it might help your chances of getting admitted. But if interviews are optional and you have found you don't come across well in interviews, skip it.

When you narrow down your list of prospective schools, you might find that you can save on airfare and other expenses by getting a great deal of information about the prospective schools on a computer. Many business schools offer through their web sites a virtual tour of their school and campus. Some of these web sites allow you to see physical facilities, classes, assignments, lists of required readings, etc. Often, business schools make videotapes available to prospective students.

If you do decide to visit, there's a good deal of homework you should do. First, you should read the catalog carefully and jot down any questions you have. When you have done this preliminary work, write to the admissions office and tell them you would like to spend the day visiting the campus. Suggest several possible dates, and let the admissions people indicate which date is best.

Keep in mind that there are different officers in charge of various areas so you may have to see three or four people to get all your questions answered. Also, ask if the school has a guided tour you can take to see what the campus is like.

Here are some questions that should be mandatory for any campus visit:

1. What are your chances of being admitted?
2. What majors are possible?
3. What is a recommended first-year program?
4. How much campus recruiting is done by companies?
5. What social activities and cultural events are available?
6. What financial aid and scholarships or assistantship opportunities are offered?

Also, be sure to:

1. See the classroom and lecture facilities.
2. Visit the business library.
3. Check on student living and dining accommodations.
4. Check on college guidance and placement facilities.

Another way to size up the various schools is to attend one of the MBA forums or similar events that are held in cities throughout the country. For example, more than 50 business schools participated in MBA forums held in several cities throughout the country a year ago. MBA forums are also held overseas. In addition, forums have been held in Hong Kong, Tokyo, Seoul, and Shanghai. Prospective students have a chance to talk with the admissions staff from many schools all at one location. It represents a substantial savings in time and money for the would-be graduate student. The Kellogg Graduate School of Management offers foreign students the chance to talk to school officials through their worldwide alumni network.

Another good idea is to see if you can locate alumni of the school from among your family's friends and acquaintances. However, try to talk to fairly recent graduates. If you discuss the school with alumni who are 20 to 30 years out of school, they may be out of touch with the philosophy and methods their alma mater now follows.

PERSONAL INTERVIEWS

If you decide to go on an interview, it could be the opportunity you need. If you are interviewed regarding admission, be sure not to ask questions that you could easily have answered by reading the college catalog. These types of questions can be a liability. Concentrate on questions that are important. In the process, be sure to give the interviewer enough insight as to your interests, academic record, and job goals to make a favorable impression.

Prior to the interview, be prepared to articulate your reasons for pursuing a graduate business degree and your interest in that particular school. It turns off many admissions officers if it appears you are interested in getting into any one of several graduate business schools and not just the one for which you are being interviewed. When asked about goals, have some clearly in mind. School officials know that everybody won't become president of a major corporation, but they would like to have some idea of your aspirations.

Finally, dress can be an important factor in the impression you make on the interviewer. Go on the assumption that dressing like a businessperson is appropriate at a business school interview.

Taking the GMAT— A Sample Exam

The GMAT score is an important factor in determining whether you get into the business school you want. Nearly all business schools require it, so make it a must. However, some years ago, Harvard dropped the requirement that all applicants must take the GMAT. The GMAT is a four-hour test that measures certain capabilities important in the study of business at the graduate level. There are both verbal and quantitative sections. Keep in mind that you are not required to have an undergraduate preparation in business to take the test. Also, international students should keep in mind that this test is *given only in English*.

Locations

The test is offered on several Saturdays during the year. If religious convictions prevent you from taking a test on Saturdays, you may request a Monday test. The test is given at centers throughout the world, and you can get a list of these from Graduate Management Admission Test, Educational Testing Service, P.O. Box 6103, Princeton, NJ 08541-6103.

You can arrange to take the test at one of the locations listed on the MBA Explorer web site at *http://www.gmat.org* and in the *GMAT Information Bulletin* available from GMAT's address in Princeton. Once you pick a testing location, simply call 800-462-8669 to schedule a date for your test. It is best to schedule the day of your choice as soon as you can because the most popular times are booked quickly.

Registration

Early registration is advised, because the center at which you request the examination may be filled and you would then be assigned to a less convenient center or be unable to take the test on the date you wish.

Before the test date, you will receive your admission ticket to the assigned test center. Be sure to check where you are to go, as sometimes you do not receive the test center you requested. When you go to the center, be sure to bring some positive identification with your photograph and signature on it.

The registration form for the GMAT comes with an explanatory booklet and complete instructions for filling out the application form, as well as sample test questions. On the test, it is best not to guess at answers about which you know nothing, as grading is done on the basis of one point for each right answer minus one quarter point for each wrong answer. The test is designed so that the average candidate will answer about two-thirds of the questions correctly.

Scores

You will receive your test scores immediately. These scores will be sent without charge to up to five graduate business schools you designate. If you want scores to be sent to other schools then or at a later date, you will be charged a fee per extra school.

There are three test scores given on your report: verbal, quantitative, and total. Verbal and quantitative scores are reported on scales that range from 0 to 60, and the total score is reported on a scale of 200 to 800. (Scores below 250 and above 700 are fairly rare; two-thirds of all candidates score between 360 and 510). You will also receive a percentile rank for each score, which will tell you the percentage of candidates that scored below you. These percentages are based on scores from all students who have taken the test during the past three years.

One big advantage of the test is that, unlike college grades, it provides the same standards for all who take it. Usually, a student who comes from a college with high grading standards is at a disadvantage compared to a student who comes from a school with low grading standards. The GMAT test helps even out these differences. Keep in mind, though, that this test is but one of the criteria for admission. Indeed, an admissions officer may discount mediocre GMAT scores if they are counterbalanced by high grades.

If you are still an undergraduate when you take your test and are not confident about your score, you may find it helpful to go over the test scores with your academic adviser. He or she may have some idea as to how your test score will affect your chances of being admitted to a given school and can suggest other schools that might be more suited to your capabilities.

Does it pay to take the test over in the hopes of boosting your scores? There is no problem with taking the test a second time, although experience shows that students repeating the test usually do not see significant changes in their scores from the first test. The average increase for students retaking the test is about 30 points. The score report on each candidate will contain the three previous GMAT scores, and these may very well be averaged together by the school to which you are applying.

Computer Adaptive

The GMAT is a computer-adaptive test (CAT), and is not administered as a paper-and-pencil exam. It is available year-round in hundreds of locations around the world, and requires only minimal computer skills.

Here are some of the advantages of the CAT.

1. Take the test when you're ready instead of having to pick from only four dates.
2. Enjoy a quiet cubicle for one, not a crowded testing room with 199 other people.
3. Phone in your registration.
4. Concentrate on one question at a time.
5. Get your quantitative and verbal scores immediately, not after weeks of waiting.

In the CAT, the computer screen displays one question at a time, chosen from a very large pool of questions organized by their content and level of difficulty. The first question in a computer-adaptive test is always of medium difficulty. The questions that follow are determined by your responses to all previous questions.

The CAT adjusts to your ability level—you'll get few questions that are either too easy or too difficult. You must enter an answer for each question, and you may not return to or change your response to any previously answered question. If you guess or answer a question incorrectly by mistake, your answers to the questions that follow will lead you back to the questions that are the appropriate level of difficulty for you.

With the GMAT on computer, test-taking strategies will have to be changed, and students will have to be somewhat familiar with using computers. More information about the GMAT is available from Educational Testing Service at 609-771-7330, fax 609-883-4349, or P.O. Box 6101, Princeton, NJ 08541-6101.

Preparation

There are special courses available to better prepare you for the GMAT and these are offered in several major cities. Much of the course work reviews questions on previous tests. If you are interested, a college adviser can tell you where and when such courses are available. One very good way to prepare for the test is to get Barron's *How to Prepare for the Graduate Management Admission Test (GMAT)* by Eugene D. Jaffe and Stephen Hilbert. You might also find a local review course worth attending if it isn't too expensive. Some colleges offer review sessions for seniors to help them prepare for the GMAT exam.

A logical first step in preparing for the GMAT is to become as familiar as possible with the types of questions that usually appear on this exam. The following analysis of typical GMAT questions explains the purpose behind each type and the best method for answering it.

ANALYTICAL WRITING ASSESSMENT

The Analytical Writing Assessment section is designed to assess your ability to think critically and to communicate complex ideas. The writing task consists of two sections that require you to examine the composition of an issue, take a position on the basis of the details of the issue, and present a critique of the conclusion derived from a specific way of thinking. The issues are taken from topics of general interest related to business or to other subjects. There is no presumption of any specific knowledge about business or other areas.

There are two types of Analytical Writing Assessment tasks.

1. **Analysis of an Issue.**
2. **Analysis of an Argument.**

READING COMPREHENSION

The Reading Comprehension section tests your ability to analyze written information and includes passages from the humanities, the social sciences, and the physical and biological sciences. The typical Reading Comprehension section consists of a passage with a total of approximately 11 questions. You will be allowed to scroll through the passages when answering the questions. However, many of the questions may be based on what is *implied* in the passages, rather than on what is explicitly stated. Your ability to draw inferences from the material is critical to successfully completing this section. You are to select the best answer from five alternatives.

There are nine types of Reading Comprehension questions.

1. **Main Idea.** You may be asked about the main idea or theme of the passage, about a possible title, or about the author's primary objective.
2. **Supporting Ideas.** You may be asked about the idea expressed in one part of the passage, rather than about the passage as a whole.
3. **Drawing Inferences.** Questions of this sort ask about ideas that are not explicitly stated in the passage.
4. **Specific Details.** You may be asked about specific facts or details the author has stated explicitly in the passage.
5. **Applying Information from the Passage to Other Situations.** These questions ask you to make an analogy between a situation described in the passage and a similar situation or event listed in the question.
6. **Tone or Attitude of the Passage.** These questions concentrate on the author's style, attitude, or mood.
7. **Technique Used by the Author in the Passage.**
8. **The Logical Structure of the Passage.** These questions test your understanding of the overall meaning, logic, or organization of the passage.
9. **Determining the Meaning of Words from the Context.**

SENTENCE CORRECTION

The Sentence Correction part of the exam tests your understanding of the basic rules of English grammar and usage. To succeed in this section, you need a command of sentence structure including tense and mood, subject and verb agreement, proper case, parallel structure, and other basics. No attempt is made to test for punctuation, spelling, or capitalization.

CRITICAL REASONING

The Critical Reasoning section of the GMAT is designed to test your ability to evaluate an assumption, inference, or argument. Each question consists of a short statement followed by a question or assumption about the statement. Each question or assumption has five possible answers. Your task is to evaluate each of the five possible choices and select the best one.

There are three different question types.

1. **Inference or Assumption.** These questions test your ability to evaluate an assumption, inference, or argument.
2. **Flaws.** You are asked to choose the best alternative answer that either represents a flaw in the statement position or, if true, would weaken the argument or conclusion.
3. **Statements of Fact.** You will be asked to find the answer that best agrees with, summarizes, or completes the statement.

PROBLEM SOLVING

The Problem Solving section of the GMAT is designed to test your ability to work with numbers. There are a variety of questions in this section dealing with the basic principles of arithmetic, algebra, and geometry. These questions may take the form of word problems or require straight calculation. In addition, questions involving the interpretation of tables and graphs may be included.

Long-term Strategy for Problem Solving

1. **Practice arithmetic.** *You cannot use a calculator on the GMAT,* so practice your arithmetic before you take the exam.
2. **Try to think quantitatively.** If you want to be a good reader, you should read a lot. In the same way, if you want to improve your quantitative skills, you should exercise them frequently.

DATA SUFFICIENCY

This type of question, which also appears in the Quantitative section, is designed to test your reasoning ability. Each Data Sufficiency question consists of a mathematical problem and two statements containing information relating to it. You must decide whether the problem can be solved by using information from: (A) the first statement alone, but not the second statement alone; (B) the second statement alone, but not the first statement alone; (C) both statements together, but neither alone; or (D) either of the statements alone. Choose (E) if the problem cannot be solved, even by using both statements together. About 40 percent of the questions on a Quantitative test will be Data Sufficiency problems.

A systematic analysis can improve your score on Data Sufficiency sections. By answering three questions, you will always arrive at the correct choice. Try to eliminate at least one of the possible choices so you can make an intelligent guess:

1. Is the first statement alone sufficient to solve the problem?
2. Is the second statement alone sufficient to solve the problem?
3. Are both statements together sufficient to solve the problem?

As a general rule try to answer the questions in order 1, 2, 3, since in many cases you will not have to answer all three to get the correct choice.

Here is how to use the three questions:

If the answer to 1 is YES, then the only possible choices are (A) or (D). Now, if the answer to 2 is YES, the choice must be (D), and if the answer to 2 is NO, the choice must be (A).

If the answer to 1 is NO, then the only possible choices are (B), (C), or (E). Now, if the answer to 2 is YES, then the choice must be (B), and if the answer to 2 is NO, the only possible choices are (C) or (E).

Finally, if the answer to 3 is YES, the choice is (C), and if the answer to 3 is NO, the choice is (E).

Sample Test

The following sample GMAT with explained answers is included here to further acquaint you with the exam. Take it under timed conditions, and carefully study the explained answers.

Answer Sheet
SAMPLE TEST

Section 1

1 Ⓐ Ⓑ Ⓒ Ⓓ Ⓔ	6 Ⓐ Ⓑ Ⓒ Ⓓ Ⓔ	11 Ⓐ Ⓑ Ⓒ Ⓓ Ⓔ	16 Ⓐ Ⓑ Ⓒ Ⓓ Ⓔ	21 Ⓐ Ⓑ Ⓒ Ⓓ Ⓔ
2 Ⓐ Ⓑ Ⓒ Ⓓ Ⓔ	7 Ⓐ Ⓑ Ⓒ Ⓓ Ⓔ	12 Ⓐ Ⓑ Ⓒ Ⓓ Ⓔ	17 Ⓐ Ⓑ Ⓒ Ⓓ Ⓔ	22 Ⓐ Ⓑ Ⓒ Ⓓ Ⓔ
3 Ⓐ Ⓑ Ⓒ Ⓓ Ⓔ	8 Ⓐ Ⓑ Ⓒ Ⓓ Ⓔ	13 Ⓐ Ⓑ Ⓒ Ⓓ Ⓔ	18 Ⓐ Ⓑ Ⓒ Ⓓ Ⓔ	23 Ⓐ Ⓑ Ⓒ Ⓓ Ⓔ
4 Ⓐ Ⓑ Ⓒ Ⓓ Ⓔ	9 Ⓐ Ⓑ Ⓒ Ⓓ Ⓔ	14 Ⓐ Ⓑ Ⓒ Ⓓ Ⓔ	19 Ⓐ Ⓑ Ⓒ Ⓓ Ⓔ	24 Ⓐ Ⓑ Ⓒ Ⓓ Ⓔ
5 Ⓐ Ⓑ Ⓒ Ⓓ Ⓔ	10 Ⓐ Ⓑ Ⓒ Ⓓ Ⓔ	15 Ⓐ Ⓑ Ⓒ Ⓓ Ⓔ	20 Ⓐ Ⓑ Ⓒ Ⓓ Ⓔ	25 Ⓐ Ⓑ Ⓒ Ⓓ Ⓔ

Section 2

1 Ⓐ Ⓑ Ⓒ Ⓓ Ⓔ	6 Ⓐ Ⓑ Ⓒ Ⓓ Ⓔ	11 Ⓐ Ⓑ Ⓒ Ⓓ Ⓔ	16 Ⓐ Ⓑ Ⓒ Ⓓ Ⓔ	21 Ⓐ Ⓑ Ⓒ Ⓓ Ⓔ
2 Ⓐ Ⓑ Ⓒ Ⓓ Ⓔ	7 Ⓐ Ⓑ Ⓒ Ⓓ Ⓔ	12 Ⓐ Ⓑ Ⓒ Ⓓ Ⓔ	17 Ⓐ Ⓑ Ⓒ Ⓓ Ⓔ	22 Ⓐ Ⓑ Ⓒ Ⓓ Ⓔ
3 Ⓐ Ⓑ Ⓒ Ⓓ Ⓔ	8 Ⓐ Ⓑ Ⓒ Ⓓ Ⓔ	13 Ⓐ Ⓑ Ⓒ Ⓓ Ⓔ	18 Ⓐ Ⓑ Ⓒ Ⓓ Ⓔ	23 Ⓐ Ⓑ Ⓒ Ⓓ Ⓔ
4 Ⓐ Ⓑ Ⓒ Ⓓ Ⓔ	9 Ⓐ Ⓑ Ⓒ Ⓓ Ⓔ	14 Ⓐ Ⓑ Ⓒ Ⓓ Ⓔ	19 Ⓐ Ⓑ Ⓒ Ⓓ Ⓔ	24 Ⓐ Ⓑ Ⓒ Ⓓ Ⓔ
5 Ⓐ Ⓑ Ⓒ Ⓓ Ⓔ	10 Ⓐ Ⓑ Ⓒ Ⓓ Ⓔ	15 Ⓐ Ⓑ Ⓒ Ⓓ Ⓔ	20 Ⓐ Ⓑ Ⓒ Ⓓ Ⓔ	25 Ⓐ Ⓑ Ⓒ Ⓓ Ⓔ

Section 3

1 Ⓐ Ⓑ Ⓒ Ⓓ Ⓔ	6 Ⓐ Ⓑ Ⓒ Ⓓ Ⓔ	11 Ⓐ Ⓑ Ⓒ Ⓓ Ⓔ	16 Ⓐ Ⓑ Ⓒ Ⓓ Ⓔ	21 Ⓐ Ⓑ Ⓒ Ⓓ Ⓔ
2 Ⓐ Ⓑ Ⓒ Ⓓ Ⓔ	7 Ⓐ Ⓑ Ⓒ Ⓓ Ⓔ	12 Ⓐ Ⓑ Ⓒ Ⓓ Ⓔ	17 Ⓐ Ⓑ Ⓒ Ⓓ Ⓔ	22 Ⓐ Ⓑ Ⓒ Ⓓ Ⓔ
3 Ⓐ Ⓑ Ⓒ Ⓓ Ⓔ	8 Ⓐ Ⓑ Ⓒ Ⓓ Ⓔ	13 Ⓐ Ⓑ Ⓒ Ⓓ Ⓔ	18 Ⓐ Ⓑ Ⓒ Ⓓ Ⓔ	23 Ⓐ Ⓑ Ⓒ Ⓓ Ⓔ
4 Ⓐ Ⓑ Ⓒ Ⓓ Ⓔ	9 Ⓐ Ⓑ Ⓒ Ⓓ Ⓔ	14 Ⓐ Ⓑ Ⓒ Ⓓ Ⓔ	19 Ⓐ Ⓑ Ⓒ Ⓓ Ⓔ	24 Ⓐ Ⓑ Ⓒ Ⓓ Ⓔ
5 Ⓐ Ⓑ Ⓒ Ⓓ Ⓔ	10 Ⓐ Ⓑ Ⓒ Ⓓ Ⓔ	15 Ⓐ Ⓑ Ⓒ Ⓓ Ⓔ	20 Ⓐ Ⓑ Ⓒ Ⓓ Ⓔ	25 Ⓐ Ⓑ Ⓒ Ⓓ Ⓔ

Section 4

1 Ⓐ Ⓑ Ⓒ Ⓓ Ⓔ	6 Ⓐ Ⓑ Ⓒ Ⓓ Ⓔ	11 Ⓐ Ⓑ Ⓒ Ⓓ Ⓔ	16 Ⓐ Ⓑ Ⓒ Ⓓ Ⓔ	21 Ⓐ Ⓑ Ⓒ Ⓓ Ⓔ
2 Ⓐ Ⓑ Ⓒ Ⓓ Ⓔ	7 Ⓐ Ⓑ Ⓒ Ⓓ Ⓔ	12 Ⓐ Ⓑ Ⓒ Ⓓ Ⓔ	17 Ⓐ Ⓑ Ⓒ Ⓓ Ⓔ	22 Ⓐ Ⓑ Ⓒ Ⓓ Ⓔ
3 Ⓐ Ⓑ Ⓒ Ⓓ Ⓔ	8 Ⓐ Ⓑ Ⓒ Ⓓ Ⓔ	13 Ⓐ Ⓑ Ⓒ Ⓓ Ⓔ	18 Ⓐ Ⓑ Ⓒ Ⓓ Ⓔ	23 Ⓐ Ⓑ Ⓒ Ⓓ Ⓔ
4 Ⓐ Ⓑ Ⓒ Ⓓ Ⓔ	9 Ⓐ Ⓑ Ⓒ Ⓓ Ⓔ	14 Ⓐ Ⓑ Ⓒ Ⓓ Ⓔ	19 Ⓐ Ⓑ Ⓒ Ⓓ Ⓔ	24 Ⓐ Ⓑ Ⓒ Ⓓ Ⓔ
5 Ⓐ Ⓑ Ⓒ Ⓓ Ⓔ	10 Ⓐ Ⓑ Ⓒ Ⓓ Ⓔ	15 Ⓐ Ⓑ Ⓒ Ⓓ Ⓔ	20 Ⓐ Ⓑ Ⓒ Ⓓ Ⓔ	25 Ⓐ Ⓑ Ⓒ Ⓓ Ⓔ

Section 5

1 Ⓐ Ⓑ Ⓒ Ⓓ Ⓔ	6 Ⓐ Ⓑ Ⓒ Ⓓ Ⓔ	11 Ⓐ Ⓑ Ⓒ Ⓓ Ⓔ	16 Ⓐ Ⓑ Ⓒ Ⓓ Ⓔ	21 Ⓐ Ⓑ Ⓒ Ⓓ Ⓔ
2 Ⓐ Ⓑ Ⓒ Ⓓ Ⓔ	7 Ⓐ Ⓑ Ⓒ Ⓓ Ⓔ	12 Ⓐ Ⓑ Ⓒ Ⓓ Ⓔ	17 Ⓐ Ⓑ Ⓒ Ⓓ Ⓔ	22 Ⓐ Ⓑ Ⓒ Ⓓ Ⓔ
3 Ⓐ Ⓑ Ⓒ Ⓓ Ⓔ	8 Ⓐ Ⓑ Ⓒ Ⓓ Ⓔ	13 Ⓐ Ⓑ Ⓒ Ⓓ Ⓔ	18 Ⓐ Ⓑ Ⓒ Ⓓ Ⓔ	23 Ⓐ Ⓑ Ⓒ Ⓓ Ⓔ
4 Ⓐ Ⓑ Ⓒ Ⓓ Ⓔ	9 Ⓐ Ⓑ Ⓒ Ⓓ Ⓔ	14 Ⓐ Ⓑ Ⓒ Ⓓ Ⓔ	19 Ⓐ Ⓑ Ⓒ Ⓓ Ⓔ	24 Ⓐ Ⓑ Ⓒ Ⓓ Ⓔ
5 Ⓐ Ⓑ Ⓒ Ⓓ Ⓔ	10 Ⓐ Ⓑ Ⓒ Ⓓ Ⓔ	15 Ⓐ Ⓑ Ⓒ Ⓓ Ⓔ	20 Ⓐ Ⓑ Ⓒ Ⓓ Ⓔ	25 Ⓐ Ⓑ Ⓒ Ⓓ Ⓔ

Section 6

1 Ⓐ Ⓑ Ⓒ Ⓓ Ⓔ	6 Ⓐ Ⓑ Ⓒ Ⓓ Ⓔ	11 Ⓐ Ⓑ Ⓒ Ⓓ Ⓔ	16 Ⓐ Ⓑ Ⓒ Ⓓ Ⓔ	21 Ⓐ Ⓑ Ⓒ Ⓓ Ⓔ
2 Ⓐ Ⓑ Ⓒ Ⓓ Ⓔ	7 Ⓐ Ⓑ Ⓒ Ⓓ Ⓔ	12 Ⓐ Ⓑ Ⓒ Ⓓ Ⓔ	17 Ⓐ Ⓑ Ⓒ Ⓓ Ⓔ	22 Ⓐ Ⓑ Ⓒ Ⓓ Ⓔ
3 Ⓐ Ⓑ Ⓒ Ⓓ Ⓔ	8 Ⓐ Ⓑ Ⓒ Ⓓ Ⓔ	13 Ⓐ Ⓑ Ⓒ Ⓓ Ⓔ	18 Ⓐ Ⓑ Ⓒ Ⓓ Ⓔ	23 Ⓐ Ⓑ Ⓒ Ⓓ Ⓔ
4 Ⓐ Ⓑ Ⓒ Ⓓ Ⓔ	9 Ⓐ Ⓑ Ⓒ Ⓓ Ⓔ	14 Ⓐ Ⓑ Ⓒ Ⓓ Ⓔ	19 Ⓐ Ⓑ Ⓒ Ⓓ Ⓔ	24 Ⓐ Ⓑ Ⓒ Ⓓ Ⓔ
5 Ⓐ Ⓑ Ⓒ Ⓓ Ⓔ	10 Ⓐ Ⓑ Ⓒ Ⓓ Ⓔ	15 Ⓐ Ⓑ Ⓒ Ⓓ Ⓔ	20 Ⓐ Ⓑ Ⓒ Ⓓ Ⓔ	25 Ⓐ Ⓑ Ⓒ Ⓓ Ⓔ

Section 7

1 Ⓐ Ⓑ Ⓒ Ⓓ Ⓔ	6 Ⓐ Ⓑ Ⓒ Ⓓ Ⓔ	11 Ⓐ Ⓑ Ⓒ Ⓓ Ⓔ	16 Ⓐ Ⓑ Ⓒ Ⓓ Ⓔ	21 Ⓐ Ⓑ Ⓒ Ⓓ Ⓔ
2 Ⓐ Ⓑ Ⓒ Ⓓ Ⓔ	7 Ⓐ Ⓑ Ⓒ Ⓓ Ⓔ	12 Ⓐ Ⓑ Ⓒ Ⓓ Ⓔ	17 Ⓐ Ⓑ Ⓒ Ⓓ Ⓔ	22 Ⓐ Ⓑ Ⓒ Ⓓ Ⓔ
3 Ⓐ Ⓑ Ⓒ Ⓓ Ⓔ	8 Ⓐ Ⓑ Ⓒ Ⓓ Ⓔ	13 Ⓐ Ⓑ Ⓒ Ⓓ Ⓔ	18 Ⓐ Ⓑ Ⓒ Ⓓ Ⓔ	23 Ⓐ Ⓑ Ⓒ Ⓓ Ⓔ
4 Ⓐ Ⓑ Ⓒ Ⓓ Ⓔ	9 Ⓐ Ⓑ Ⓒ Ⓓ Ⓔ	14 Ⓐ Ⓑ Ⓒ Ⓓ Ⓔ	19 Ⓐ Ⓑ Ⓒ Ⓓ Ⓔ	24 Ⓐ Ⓑ Ⓒ Ⓓ Ⓔ
5 Ⓐ Ⓑ Ⓒ Ⓓ Ⓔ	10 Ⓐ Ⓑ Ⓒ Ⓓ Ⓔ	15 Ⓐ Ⓑ Ⓒ Ⓓ Ⓔ	20 Ⓐ Ⓑ Ⓒ Ⓓ Ⓔ	25 Ⓐ Ⓑ Ⓒ Ⓓ Ⓔ

Cut along dashed line to remove answer sheet

SAMPLE TEST
with Answers and Analysis

Writing Assessment

Part I
TIME: 30 minutes

<u>Directions:</u> Write a clear, logical, and well-organized response to the following issue or argument. Your response should be in the form of a short essay, following the conventions of standard written English. Your answer should fit on three pages of lined 8½" × 11" paper or equivalent on your PC. Write legibly. Essays that are illegible or that are written on a topic other than the one outlined in the question will not be scored.

Forced obsolescence is a strategy that manufacturers use to limit the useful life of some consumer products in order to increase sales. Some commentators complain that this practice results in a waste of resources. What they do not understand is that by shortening the life cycle of products, manufacturers are able to both improve them and lower the cost to the consumer.

Which statement do you find more convincing, that forced obsolescence wastes resources or that it benefits consumers? State your position using relevant reasons from your own experience, observation, or reading.

Part II
TIME: 30 minutes

<u>Directions:</u> Write a clear, logical, and well-organized response to the following issue or argument. Your response should be in the form of a short essay, following the conventions of standard written English. Your answer should fit on three pages of lined 8½" × 11" paper or equivalent on your PC. Write legibly. Essays that are illegible or that are written on a topic other than the one outlined in the question will not be scored.

Women are more fashion conscious than men. Women's clothing styles change every year, forcing them to update their wardrobes so as not to appear behind the times.

Discuss how logically persuasive you find the above argument. In presenting your point of view, analyze the sort of reasoning used and its supporting evidence. In addition, state what further evidence, if any, would make the argument more sound and convincing or would make you better able to evaluate its conclusion.

STOP
IF THERE IS STILL TIME REMAINING, YOU MAY REVIEW YOUR ANSWER. AFTER YOU HAVE CONFIRMED YOUR ANSWER, YOU CANNOT RETURN TO THIS QUESTION.

Reprinted from Barron's *How to Prepare for the GMAT*, 11th edition, by Eugene D. Jaffe and Stephen Hilbert, © 1998 by Barron's Educational Series, Inc.

1 1 1 1 1 1 1 1 1 1 1

Section 1

TIME: 30 minutes
25 Questions

<u>Directions:</u> This part contains three reading passages. You are to read each one carefully. When answering the questions, you *will* be allowed to refer back to the passages. The questions are based on what is *stated* or *implied* in each passage.

Passage 1:

The following passage was written in 1964.

The main burden of assuring that the resources of the federal government are well managed falls on relatively few of the five million men and women
Line whom it employs. Under the department and agency
(5) heads there are 8,600 political, career, military, and foreign service executives—the top managers and professionals—who exert major influence on the manner in which the rest are directed and utilized. Below their level there are other thousands with
(10) assignments of some managerial significance, but we believe that the line of demarcation selected is the best available for our purposes in this attainment.

In addition to Presidential appointees in responsible posts, the 8,600 include the three highest
(15) grades under the Classification Act; the three highest grades in the postal field service; comparable grades in the foreign service; general officers in the military service; and similar classes in other special services and in agencies or positions
(20) excepted from the Classification Act.

There is no complete inventory of positions or people in federal service at this level. The lack may be explained by separate agency statutes and personnel systems, diffusion among so many
(25) special services, and absence of any central point (short of the President himself) with jurisdiction over all upper-level personnel of the government.

This Committee considers establishment and maintenance of a central inventory of these key
(30) people and positions to be an elementary necessity, a first step in improved management throughout the Executive Branch.

Top Presidential appointees, about 500 of them, bear the brunt of translating the philosophy and aims
(35) of the current administration into practical programs.

This group includes the secretaries and assistant secretaries of cabinet departments, agency heads and their deputies, heads and members of boards and commissions with fixed terms, and chiefs and
(40) directors of major bureaus, divisions, and services. Appointments to many of these politically sensitive positions are made on recommendation by department or agency heads, but all are presumably responsible to Presidential leadership.

(45) One qualification for office at this level is that there be no basic disagreement with Presidential political philosophy, at least so far as administrative judgments and actions are concerned. Apart from the bi-partisan boards and commissions, these
(50) men are normally identified with the political party of the President, or are sympathetic to it, although there are exceptions.

There are four distinguishable kinds of top Presidential appointees, including:

(55) —Those whom the President selects at the outset to establish immediate and effective control over the government (e.g., Cabinet secretaries, agency heads, his own White House staff and Executive Office Personnel).

(60) —Those selected by department and agency heads in order to establish control within their respective organizations (e.g.—assistant secretaries, deputies, assistants to, and major line posts in some bureaus and divisions).

(65) —High-level appointees who—though often requiring clearance through political or interest group channels, or both—must have known scientific or technical competence (e.g.—the Surgeon General, the Commissioner of
(70) Education).

GO ON TO THE NEXT PAGE ➤

1 1 1 1 1 1 1 1 1 1 1 1

—Those named to residual positions traditionally filled on a partisan patronage basis.

These appointees are primarily regarded as policy makers and overseers of policy execution. In (75) practice, however, they usually have substantial responsibilities in line management, often requiring a thorough knowledge of substantive agency programs.

1. According to the passage, about how many top managerial professionals work for the federal government?

(A) 5 million
(B) 2 million
(C) 20 thousand
(D) 9 thousand
(E) 5 hundred

2. No complete inventory exists of positions in the three highest levels of government service because

(A) no one has bothered to count them
(B) computers cannot handle all the data
(C) separate agency personnel systems are used
(D) the President has never requested such information
(E) the Classification Act prohibits such a census

3. Top Presidential appointees have as their central responsibility the

(A) prevention of politically motivated interference with the actions of their agencies
(B) monitoring of government actions on behalf of the President's own political party
(C) translation of the aims of the administration into practical programs
(D) investigation of charges of corruption within the government
(E) maintenance of adequate controls over the rate of government spending

4. One exception to the general rule that top Presidential appointees must be in agreement with the President's political philosophy may be found in

(A) most cabinet-level officers
(B) members of the White House staff
(C) bi-partisan boards and commissions
(D) those offices filled on a patronage basis
(E) offices requiring scientific or technical expertise

5. Applicants for Presidential appointments are usually identified with or are members of

(A) large corporations
(B) the foreign service
(C) government bureaus
(D) academic circles
(E) the President's political party

6. Appointees that are selected directly by the President include

(A) U.S. marshals and attorneys
(B) military officers
(C) agency heads
(D) assistant secretaries
(E) congressional committee members

7. Appointees usually have to possess expertise in

(A) line management
(B) military affairs
(C) foreign affairs
(D) strategic planning
(E) constitutional law

8. According to the passage, Presidential appointees are regarded primarily as

(A) political spokespeople
(B) policy makers
(C) staff managers
(D) scientific or technical experts
(E) business executives

9. Appointees selected by department and agency heads include

(A) military leaders
(B) cabinet secretaries
(C) deputy secretaries
(D) diplomats
(E) residual position holders

GO ON TO THE NEXT PAGE ➤

Passage 2:

The first and decisive step in the expansion of
Europe overseas was the conquest of the Atlantic
Ocean. That the nation to achieve this should be
Line Portugal was the logical outcome of her geographi-
(5) cal position and her history. Placed on the extreme
margin of the old, classical Mediterranean world
and facing the untraversed ocean, Portugal could
adapt and develop the knowledge and experience
of the past to meet the challenge of the unknown.
(10) Some centuries of navigating the coastal waters of
Western Europe and Northern Africa had prepared
Portuguese seamen to appreciate the problems
which the Ocean presented and to apply and
develop the methods necessary to overcome them.
(15) From the seamen of the Mediterranean, particularly
those of Genoa and Venice, they had learned the
organization and conduct of a mercantile marine,
and from Jewish astronomers and Catalan
mapmakers the rudiments of navigation. Largely
(20) excluded from a share in Mediterranean commerce
at a time when her increasing and vigorous
population was making heavy demands on her
resources, Portugal turned southwards and west-
wards for opportunities of trade and commerce. At
(25) this moment of national destiny it was fortunate for
her that in men of the calibre of Prince Henry,
known as the Navigator, and King John II she
found resolute and dedicated leaders.

The problems to be faced were new and com-
(30) plex. The conditions for navigation and commerce
in the Mediterranean were relatively simple,
compared with those in the western seas. The
landlocked Mediterranean, tideless and with a
climatic regime of regular and well-defined
(35) seasons, presented few obstacles to sailors who
were the heirs of a great body of sea lore garnered
from the experiences of many centuries. What
hazards there were, in the form of sudden storms or
dangerous coasts, were known and could be
(40) usually anticipated. Similarly the Mediterranean
coasts, though they might be for long periods in the
hands of dangerous rivals, were described in
sailing directions or laid down on the portolan
charts drawn by Venetian, Genoese and Catalan
(45) cartographers. Problems of determining positions
at sea, which confronted the Portuguese, did not
arise. Though the Mediterranean seamen by no
means restricted themselves to coastal sailing, the
latitudinal extent of the Mediterranean was not

(50) great, and voyages could be conducted from point
to point on compass bearings; the ships were never
so far from land as to make it necessary to fix their
positions in latitude by astronomical observations.
Having made a landfall on a bearing, they could
(55) determine their precise position from prominent
landmarks, soundings or the nature of the sea bed,
after reference to the sailing directions or charts.

By contrast, the pioneers of ocean navigation
faced much greater difficulties. The western ocean
(60) which extended, according to the speculations of
the cosmographers, through many degrees of
latitude and longitude, was an unknown quantity,
but certainly subjected to wide variations of
weather and without known bounds. Those who
(65) first ventured out over its waters did so without
benefit of sailing directions or traditional lore. As
the Portuguese sailed southwards, they left behind
them the familiar constellations in the heavens by
which they could determine direction and the hours
(70) of the night, and particularly the pole-star from
which by a simple operation they could determine
their latitude. Along the unknown coasts they were
threatened by shallows, hidden banks, rocks and
contrary winds and currents, with no knowledge of
(75) convenient shelter to ride out storms or of very
necessary watering places. It is little wonder that
these pioneers dreaded the thought of being forced
on to a lee shore or of having to choose between
these inshore dangers and the unrecorded perils of
(80) the open sea.

10. Before the expansion of Europe overseas could take
place

    (A) vast sums of money had to be raised
    (B) an army had to be recruited
    (C) the Atlantic Ocean had to be conquered
    (D) ships had to be built
    (E) sailors had to be trained

GO ON TO THE NEXT PAGE ➤